FEMININE APPEAL

*Seven Virtues of a
Godly Wife and Mother*

CAROLYN MAHANEY

FOREWORD BY
NANCY LEIGH DEMOSS

CROSSWAY BOOKS

A DIVISION OF
GOOD NEWS PUBLISHERS
WHEATON, ILLINOIS

Feminine Appeal

Copyright © 2003 by Carolyn Mahaney and Sovereign Grace Ministries

Published by Crossway Books
  a division of Good News Publishers
  1300 Crescent Street
  Wheaton, Illinois 60187

Cover design: Josh Dennis

Cover photo: Getty Images

First printing, 2003

Printed in the United States of America

Library of Congress Cataloging-in-Publication Data
Mahaney, Carolyn, 1955-
  Feminine appeal : seven virtues of a godly wife and mother / Carolyn
Mahaney ; foreword by Nancy Leigh DeMoss.
    p. cm.
  Includes bibliographical references.
  ISBN 1-58134-463-5 (alk. paper)
  1. Christian women—Religious life. 2. Wives—Conduct of life.
3. Mothers—Conduct of life. 4. Virtues. I. Title.
BV4527.M235   2003
248.8'435—dc21   2003005845

DP		13	12	11	10	09	08	07	06	05	04	03
15	14	13	12	11	10	9	8	7	6	5	4	3	2	1

Contents

Acknowledgments

My heartfelt thanks to:

The entire staff at Crossway Books for your genuine love for God and your bold commitment to sound doctrine. Working with you has been a sheer privilege for this inexperienced first-time author.

Mark Dever for making that phone call to Dr. Dennis (president of Crossway Books) to recommend that my "Titus 2" audiotapes be published in book form—even though you didn't ask my permission!

Lane and Ebeth Dennis for your enthusiasm over the content of the "Titus 2" tapes and for pursuing me to write a book. Never in a million years would I have dreamed that I would take up such an endeavor. I am indebted to you both for the opportunity.

Marvin Padgett for your support and patience with me throughout this project, even when I requested yet *another* extension!

Lila Bishop for your skillful editing.

Josh and Shannon Harris, Gary and Lisa Thomas, Randy and Nanci Alcorn, Grant (my special "little brother") and Karin Layman, Jeff Purswell, Mike Bullmore, Valori Maresco, Nancy Loftness, and Betsy Ricucci for your invaluable critique of the chapters you read.

The people of Covenant Life Church and Sovereign Grace Ministries for every encouraging word you shared, every loving note you wrote, and every sacrificial prayer you offered up to heaven on my behalf. You truly are "the dearest people on earth."

The CLC pastors' wives, SGM team wives, "The Crazy Ladies," and my many other faithful friends. Although I desperately missed our regular times together over this past year, your unflagging care was a bastion of strength for me. Thank you for the many letters, e-mails, gifts, Starbucks drink deliveries, meals for my family, timely encouragement, and faithful prayers that you kept coming my way. How can I thank God enough for you?

Nora Earles for the dedication and joy with which you serve C. J. and me. Though it's true that no one is indispensable, we think you are the exception!

Carolyn McCulley for enthusiastically applying your writing gift to help me transfer the "Titus 2" material into written form. Then again, that is how you approach life—seeking to use the gifts God has given you to make others a success.

My sisters, Janice Dillon and Helen Dickinson, for the heroic way you are caring for Dad and Mom during this season. In my view, your servanthood is unparalleled.

Brian, Steve, and Mike for loving your wives, my daughters. No mother has finer sons-in-law!

My three precious grandsons—Andrew, Liam, and Jack—for bringing me so much joy.

My son Chad for wanting to make the day I finished this book "a national holiday." Your excitement meant so much to me, my son! But your faithful prayers meant even more. Thank you for your love for God and His Word, for your obedience and humility, and for the affection you show your family. You make your mother's heart very glad.

My daughter Janelle. No words can ever express the gratitude I feel for the way you joyfully took responsibility for my household duties so I could be free to write. Never once did you complain, but instead constantly told me how much you loved serving me. There simply would be no book apart from your sacrifice. And thanks for making me laugh along the way. What a gift from God you are to me!

My daughter Kristin for wishing you were geographically closer so you could have practically helped me as well. Honey, I can assure you that the way you live your life blesses me even more. Thank you for how you prize your husband, tenderly love your boys, and effectively manage your home. You exemplify what is written on the pages of this book.

My daughter Nicole for accompanying and assisting me on the rigorous journey of writing—batting around ideas, hammering out issues, challenging points that didn't make sense, and painstakingly poring over every single word of this book with me. And for persevering to the finish line—only two days before giving birth to your firstborn son! Your tenacity was remarkable. Your help was incalculable. There is no way I could have completed this journey without you. I am forever grateful to you, Nicole!

My husband, C. J., for being my chief editor, my mentor, my lover, my greatest encourager, and my dearest friend.

> If ever two were one, then surely we;
> If ever man were loved by wife, then thee;
> If ever wife was happy in a man,
> Compare with me, ye women, if you can.[1]
>
> ANNE BRADSTREET, 1678

Foreword

By Nancy Leigh DeMoss

❧

As I survey the landscape of women and women's ministry in the Christian church today, I'd have to say that the view is both bleak and promising. There is cause for both grave concern and genuine hope.

First the bad news.

Christian women—no less than nonbelieving women—are in desperate need of the truth. The look of frustration, pain, or hollowness in so many eyes tells the story of women who are generally disappointed with life. They feel victimized—even traumatized—by circumstances that have fallen short of their hopes and dreams. As far as they are concerned, life just isn't working.

And the problem goes even deeper than what is obvious at first glance. I believe that this sense of confusion and distress among Christian women is because, by and large, we are profoundly disoriented about who God is and who we are, and about our calling and mission in life—*as women.* Almost *en masse* we have bought into a way of thinking about life and about womanhood, marriage, and family that is culturally accepted and politically correct but fundamentally flawed. For sure, it has not delivered what it promised.

But I said there's good news also. And there is. Everywhere I go, as I speak about the ways of God and what it means to reflect the glory of God as a woman, I am greatly encouraged by the hunger and eagerness of many women to receive the Word and to act on it.

As has always been the case, God has a "remnant"—in this case, women who have ears to hear, who resonate with the truth, and who are willing to make tough, radical choices to reorient their lives around the Word of God.

Life isn't necessarily easier for these women, but they are experiencing a sense of purpose, joy, and blessing as they see the connection between their lives and the grander scheme of the purposes of God and the kingdom of Christ.

Here's something else I find heartening: God has raised up in our day a handful of women who are grounded in the Word and understand the biblical perspective of womanhood—women who are godly role models and gifted teachers, who are committed to communicate the truth to other women with courage and compassion.

Most of these women are not high-profile individuals—they have not sought the limelight or aspired to positions of influence; rather, they have spent years faithfully loving and serving their husbands and children and applying themselves to studying and living out the Word of God. Their influence is not the result of human credentials or impressive resumes. It is the fruit of godly living and sincere devotion to Christ.

Carolyn Mahaney is one such woman. Several years ago I received an audiotape series of her teaching for women based on Titus 2. As I listened, my heart rejoiced at her evident love for the truth and her clear, compelling presentation of this passage that outlines the "curriculum" that should be at the heart of all ministry by and to women. I was delighted when Carolyn agreed to put that teaching in book form.

Carolyn is not just a theoretician. Through nearly thirty years of marriage, and as the mother of four, she has lived out the priorities and virtues of Titus 2 in the laboratory of life. And, as the Scripture directs, she is a discipler and has poured out her life to teach the ways of God to others—first to her three daughters and then to women in the church.

If you are a "younger woman," you hold in your hands a mentor, an excellent guide to spiritual maturity. This is your opportunity to sit at the feet of a woman who has been farther down the path than you and who is equipped to help you understand and embrace God's plan and purpose for your life.

Perhaps you qualify as an "older woman." You will find in this book a practical tool to help you fulfill your mandate to invest in the lives of younger women. According to Scripture, this is what you are to teach the women He puts in your life.

Feminine Appeal will help Christian women recover the nearly lost treasure of God's way of thinking and living. I pray that God will use it to give birth to a supernatural movement of revival and reformation in the hearts and homes of women in our day.

1

Transformed by Titus 2

Racing the clock in rush-hour traffic, Lisa groaned as she saw the predictable bloom of brake lights in front of her. She was going to be late again to the daycare center. An adrenaline-driven surge of anxiety erupted.

"Come on, come on, come *on!*" she hissed at the cars ahead.

Arriving ten minutes late, she mentally calculated the fine levied on tardy parents while she hoisted her son Nate into his well-worn car seat. In between her son's chatter on the way home, she tried to recall what she had purchased at the grocery store during her lunch hour. *Did I remember to put away the ice cream?* she wondered.

They arrived home only minutes before her husband, John, and their older son, Matthew. Entering the dark house, Lisa walked through the handsomely furnished rooms that sat empty all day and flicked on the overhead kitchen light. Grocery bags sat on every level surface, including the kitchen table.

One was leaking.

Dumping the melted ice cream in the trash, she popped something pre-made into the microwave. With one eye on the clock during dinner, Lisa estimated the amount of time she had to get the boys to bed and still pack for tomorrow's trip.

"Come on, guys, let's get ready for bed," she said, pointing them toward the stairs.

Nate stopped at the door to the basement, an expansive playroom outfitted with a lavish collection of toys.

"Moh-mmeee," whined the four-year-old, as he looked down the dark steps, "we didn't even get to play with our *own* toys today."

Irritation, guilt, and sympathy converged as she knelt to hug her child. Up close, she could see exhaustion spiked with contentious confusion in his face. But the schedule must go on. Up the stairs they went—the boys to bed, Lisa to her bedroom where the open suitcase sprawled on her side of the bed.

Something is very wrong here, she kept thinking to herself as she packed her bag by rote. *This isn't what the good life is supposed to feel like.* Shoes? Check. Pantyhose? Check. *But this is what I've chosen.* Umbrella? Check. Phone adapter? Check. *I'm the youngest vice president in company history. We have an impressive house in a good neighborhood.* Prescriptions? Check. Toothbrush? Check. *The boys are in the best daycare and preschool in town. We should be happy.*

Why isn't this satisfying? Why do I feel so overwhelmed?

MY GIRLHOOD DREAM

Though I have never tried to juggle a full-time job and a family like my friend Lisa, I have my own memories of being completely overwhelmed.

Growing up in sunny, rural Sarasota, Florida, my dream was to one day become a wife and mother. Shortly after graduating from high school, I worked as a secretary for a Christian organization. There I met a young, exuberant preacher from the Washington, D.C. area named C. J. Mahaney, and I soon suspected my girlhood dream might come true. Sure enough, just three months after our first meeting, he proposed. Without hesitation, I said yes.

I did not consider it a hardship that I would need to leave the place where I had lived my whole life to join my new husband in the suburbs of our nation's capital. I was not apprehensive about saying goodbye to everyone and everything I had ever known in order to be this man's wife. That is, until we got married. C. J. was twenty-one at that time. I was nineteen. I will never forget those early days as a new bride, now more than twenty-eight years ago.

Upon returning from our honeymoon, C. J. and I made our home in a tiny one-bedroom apartment. Though I loved being married, the cold winters of D.C. were not to my liking (I had never even seen snow before!). My husband and I were in love and the best of friends; however, I soon began to miss my family and friends in Florida, and new friendships were slow to develop.

But my greatest challenge—by far—was my desire to do this "wife thing" well, but I was not sure how to pull it off. I remember thinking: *I wish there were a crash course I could take for this.* I longed to have a strong, godly, joy-filled marriage, but I had seen so many marriages fail, even Christian marriages. And the couples all started out happy and in love like C. J. and me. Where did they go wrong? How could I make certain that we didn't end up in the same place?

I yearned for someone to give me direction and guidance—to share with me the essential ingredients for a successful marriage. I knew it involved more than cooking and cleaning the house. But beyond that, I wasn't sure where to begin.

The feelings of incompetence only grew stronger as children started to arrive. I became pregnant three months after our wedding. By age twenty-one, I had an infant and a one-year-old. In those first two years of marriage, there were days when I felt my battle with homesickness *and* morning sickness (more like all-day sickness) would never end. I had no prior experience caring for children, and to say the least, I felt inadequate and unprepared.

WHAT IS GOOD?

Maybe you recognize yourself in Lisa's story. You find that life is galloping by at a furious pace, and you are frantically trying to catch your breath. You wonder if you are making the right choices.

Or perhaps you identify more with my life. You are a full-time homemaker, but still you are overwhelmed by all your responsibilities. You wish you knew of a better way to carry out this enormous task.

Isn't it telling that our culture requires training and certification for so many vocations of lesser importance, but hands us marriage and motherhood without instruction? Fortunately, God hasn't left us to fend for ourselves. He has provided invaluable wisdom for women in His Word.

If we question whether we are investing our lives in what is truly important, we have received the plumb line for women straight from holy Scripture. Look at the clear instructions found in the second chapter of Titus, verses 3 to 5:

> *Older women likewise are to be reverent in behavior, not slander-ers or slaves to much wine. They are to teach what is good, and so train the young women to love their husbands and children, to be self-controlled, pure, working at home, kind, and submissive to their own husbands, that the word of God may not be reviled.*

More than any other, this section of Scripture has shaped my own understanding of biblical womanhood. This passage set the standard and provided the direction I so desperately needed in those early years of marriage. And for the past twenty-eight years, these words have guided me in my role as a wife and mother.

Not only has Titus 2 transformed my life, but I've seen it revolu-tionize the lives of countless other women. No matter what your age or season of life—whether you are a grandmother or a high school stu-dent—this passage is applicable to you.

In this book we will explore the rich, wonderful counsel that the Lord provides for women in Titus 2. One chapter each will be devoted to "what is good"—loving our husbands, loving our children, self-control, purity, working at home, kindness, and submission in mar-riage. (Did you raise your eyebrows at the mention of submission? It's not a popular word today, but stick with me, and you'll probably be surprised and encouraged by the reason the Lord listed it among "what is good.")

THE MENTORING MANDATE

The seven feminine virtues listed in Titus 2 are prefaced with a clear call to action for older women: "Teach what is good, and so train the young women."

I longed for this kind of help and instruction in my early years of marriage and motherhood. I earnestly desired to have a more experi-enced, godly woman to whom I could go for advice.

My mom was an excellent role model who made caring for a fam-ily look effortless. But she was a thousand miles away, and I couldn't contact her on a daily basis. How I wished I had paid closer attention when I lived at home!

As the first among my friends to have a baby, I had no one close by whom I could ask for help. I felt very alone in this daunting task of being a wife and mother.

I remember one unhelpful method (among many) I followed with my first child, Nicole. To keep her from crying, I would nurse (and in later months, bottle-feed) her until she fell asleep. Then I would *very carefully* lay her in bed. If she woke up in the process—which happened frequently, I might add—I would have to start the whole operation over again. This ordeal could take up to an hour and a half at every naptime and nightly bedtime. To say the least, it was an exhausting and time-consuming routine.

I continued this faulty practice until my second daughter, Kristin, was born fourteen months later. My mother was visiting to help me with the girls, and she observed my effort to care for a newborn while maintaining this bedtime practice with Nicole. "Carolyn," she admonished, "you need to put Nicole to bed and just let her cry."

I was desperate at this point; so without hesitation I followed her counsel. The first night Nicole cried for fifteen minutes. The next day for her nap, she whimpered only a few moments. That night she went to sleep without crying. To think I had spent all those months going through that arduous routine! How much time and effort would have been saved if only I had received the simple, practical advice of an older woman.

Our Titus 2 passage exhorts older women to provide this kind of assistance for young women. If you are an older woman, may I appeal to you to take up this challenge? Young women are in dire need of your training and instruction.

To function in this role you need not have the gift of teaching or be a theological expert; it simply requires you to possess proven character (as outlined in verse 3). The years have brought you much knowledge and insight, and you have a significant role to play in the church. You have discovered secrets of godly wisdom in relation to husbands, children, and the home that could save younger women a lot of unnecessary trouble and concern.

Author and speaker Elisabeth Elliot encourages older women in this way:

It would help younger women to know there are a few listening ears when they don't know what to do with an uncommunicative husband, a 25-pound turkey, or a two-year-old's tantrum.

It is doubtful that the Apostle Paul had in mind Bible classes or seminars or books when he spoke of *teaching* younger women. He meant the simple things, the everyday example, the willingness to take time from one's own concerns to pray with the anxious mother, to walk with her the way of the cross—with its tremendous demands of patience, selflessness, lovingkindness—and to show her, in the ordinariness of Monday through Saturday, how to keep a quiet heart.

These lessons will come perhaps most convincingly through rocking a baby, doing some mending, cooking a supper, or cleaning a refrigerator. Through such an example, one young woman—single or married, Christian or not—may glimpse the mystery of charity and the glory of womanhood.[1]

Of all the mentoring relationships among women, none is more significant than the one between a mother and her daughter. Those of us who have been blessed with daughters have the opportunity and, indeed, the obligation to emphasize the feminine qualities of Titus 2 in our teaching repertoire.

We must instruct them how to love their future husbands and how to love their future children, in the likely event that God has that plan for their lives. We must train them how to be self-controlled, pure, kind, workers at home, and submissive.

We live in a society that emphasizes preparation and education for everything *but* marriage, motherhood, and homemaking. Therefore, we must give this profession our highest attention when it comes to preparing our daughters for their futures.

May I also encourage those of you who are single? If marriage and motherhood are in your future, *now* is the time to prepare for that profession. Even if you remain single, you can still cultivate biblical femininity by studying this passage. It will instruct you in how to care for the marriages and children of those closest to you. You don't have to draw from personal experience; you still have the truth of God's Word to train the younger women in your life.

Clearly, Titus 2 exhorts *all* women to perceive the value of being mentored and being a mentor. Younger women should consistently pursue more mature women to learn from their wisdom and experience. Older women should prayerfully consider the younger women that God has brought into their lives, in order to encourage and support them.

A MENTORING STORY

It was the friendship and counsel of an older woman that God used to influence my friend Lisa. Though Lisa had been attending church services periodically, she didn't know the truth of the gospel and was only living for herself. However, she encountered God, and He turned her life upside down. He shook loose all her previous concepts of femininity, marriage, and motherhood. She tells her experience:

> I grew up at a time when women were making a name for themselves. In their own right, they were being promoted into the "men only" fields without the obstacles or prejudices of the past. Women were prompted to put themselves where they could make their mark. I never heard anyone talk or teach about raising a family or being a wife.
>
> In my family, I was encouraged to pursue my interests, study hard, and have a shining career. I remember in college my friends and I would talk about careers, strategies, and positions of rank. We always pictured ourselves as successful executives. I specifically recall tossing around the idea of not having children.
>
> My path into corporate America was incredibly easy. I had a wonderful job waiting for me out of college. From there the climb was more like a ride in a glass elevator. At the age of twenty-eight, I had my CPA license and found myself the comptroller of a multimillion-dollar corporation and the youngest vice president in company history.
>
> But with success came resentment that I was tied down with a family. I had to decline a promotion and an opportunity to move abroad. I had two young sons, and my husband was in a nowhere job. My family felt like the chains of Jacob Marley. I couldn't see the joy in having a family—only the glory I was missing. I was in a mental trap that I didn't perceive.

Through a series of God-ordained "coincidences," several people recommended the same church to John and Lisa. One Sunday they decided to visit, and on that day the pastor clearly presented the gospel and preached about the eternal importance of family. The message pierced Lisa's heart. Drawn by the teaching and life of the church community, they began to attend this new church. Not much later, Lisa repented of her sins and became a Christian.

Soon the conversations at work about vacations, wardrobes, and material success that she once enjoyed seemed silly and selfish. Instead Lisa began to prize the biblical roles of wife and mother. Eventually, John and Lisa agreed it was time to sell their big house, buy a less expensive place to live, and prepare for Lisa to come home full time. It took the better part of a year to sell the house, during which time she turned down a promotion that would have doubled her salary. This ordeal tested her faith.

> I struggled even as I tried to obey. I knew my life needed to be in God's ordained order. But I wondered if I could really do this.
>
> As we prepared to move, I befriended a woman in my church who helped me pack a little every day for a month. During our times together, she would listen patiently and help me in practical ways. She continually quoted Scripture, targeting my doubts. It wasn't always what I wanted to hear. Nevertheless, it was always what I *needed* to hear.
>
> My husband got a new job, one he loves to go to every day. We found a bargain home in a modest neighborhood close to our church community. I'm home with my boys. We live on less money, but we really lack nothing.
>
> But that's not even the best part. Now we are involved in each other's lives! I really know my husband and my children. My boys are learning, happy, and love the Lord, and I am already seeing the fruit of my labors.
>
> As much as the Lord has blessed our family, over the years He has also used this change in our lives to reach others. Former colleagues and disinterested family members have started asking questions about our faith and are reading the Bible. The witness of our life together even made my skeptical oldest sister comment, "Maybe there *is* something to this God thing!"

Isn't that exciting? It's the Titus 2 principle at work! One older woman in the faith mentoring a new convert and helping her make a transition to being at home, caring for her sons, and supporting her husband. In turn, Lisa is able to train and encourage other women in her church; and the transformation in her life is a witness to unbelieving family members and friends.

THE GRAND PURPOSE

Now there are many Christian women who agree with and adhere to the virtues listed in Titus 2, but are unaware of the ultimate purpose of these practical applications. These women are avid proponents of society's need to return to "traditional values;" yet that is not what this passage is advocating. We are *not* commanded to love our husbands and to love our children so we can have strong, happy families like those from a previous era. To be sure, we experience enjoyable and fruitful family relationships when we follow God's instructions. But there is a far higher call.

On the other hand, there are Christian women who reject some of these virtues because they regard them as restrictive and outdated. They single out "working at home" and "submissive to their own husbands" as purely cultural requirements that are not applicable in modern society. However, that idea is erroneous. This passage remains authoritative and relevant for women today.

The commands found in Titus 2 have been given to us for an all-important reason that transcends time and culture. *That reason is the gospel of Jesus Christ.* These virtues are not about our personal fulfillment or individual preference. They are required for the sake of unbelievers—so that those who are lost might come to know our Savior.

This purpose is stated in verses 5, 8, and 10. We are to love our husbands and children, pursue self-control and purity, be workers at home, kind and submissive:

that the word of God may not be reviled. (v. 5)

so that an opponent may be put to shame, having nothing evil to say about us. (v. 8)

so that in everything [we] may adorn the doctrine of God our Savior. (v. 10)

Our conduct has a direct influence on how people think about the gospel. The world doesn't judge us by our theology; the world judges us by our behavior. People don't necessarily want to know what we believe about the Bible. *They want to see if what we believe makes a dif-ference in our lives.* Our actions either bring honor to God or misrep-resent His truth.

I recall my sadness when I heard of a high-profile Christian woman who left her husband for another man. My heart ached when I thought of the pain that this caused her family. But the effect of her sin didn't end there. When she broke God's command and committed adultery, her behavior reviled God's Word—before every person she knew and more she didn't know. Even the mainstream media snickered at the hypocrisy they perceived in her life. Her sinful conduct gave opponents of the gospel the chance to speak evil about Christians.

Although our daily actions might not be covered on the evening news, our lifestyle speaks loudly to those around us. How sobering it is to realize that our behavior has the potential to discredit the gospel. But how exciting it is to think that we can actually *commend* the gospel!

As verse 10 says, we can "adorn" the gospel with our lives. To "adorn" means to put something beautiful or attractive on display—like placing a flawless gemstone in a setting that uniquely shows off its brilliance. The gospel is like the most valuable of jewels. It is *the pearl* of great price.

Make no mistake, by adorning the gospel, we are not enhancing or improving it. The gospel cannot be improved! But by cultivating the feminine qualities listed in Titus 2, we can present the gospel as attrac-tive, impressive, and pleasing to a watching world.

Several years ago while we were on a family outing, a gentleman approached my husband and said, "Sir, I've been observing you for some time, and I have never seen a family relate like yours. How do you do it?"

My husband and I and our children had simply been enjoying one another's company—laughing together and showing affection. But what was ordinary interaction between our family members was curi-ously attractive to this stranger. Our behavior provided C. J. the opportunity to share the gospel with him.

My husband explained that we are simply a family of sinners—but sinners whose lives have been transformed by the power of the gospel. And *that* was the reason for the difference this man observed.

Although we might not always be aware, people are watching our lives. If we exhibit the qualities from Titus 2 such as love for our families or purity or kindness, we are promoting the gospel. And the unbelievers who see us—be they family member, friend, neighbor, or stranger—may actually be drawn to the gospel by the way we live. How extraordinary!

FEMININE APPEAL

This book is about the transforming effect of the gospel—because that is what Titus 2 is all about. The climax of Titus 2 announces that "the grace of God has appeared, bringing salvation for all people." It heralds the news of "our great God and Savior Jesus Christ, who gave himself for us to redeem us from all lawlessness" (vv. 11-14).

The seven feminine virtues we will consider in this book are not an end in themselves. They point to the transforming effect of the gospel in the lives of women—women who have turned from their sins and trusted in the Savior, women whose sins have been forgiven and whose hearts have been changed.

Can you conceive of anything that sets forth the beauty of the gospel jewel more brilliantly than the godly behavior of those who have received it? Consider the loveliness of a woman who passionately adores her husband, who tenderly cherishes her children, who creates a warm and peaceful home, who exemplifies purity, self-control, and kindness in her character and who gladly submits to her husband's leadership—for all the days God grants her life. I dare say there are few things that display the gospel jewel with greater elegance. This is true *feminine appeal.*

2

The Delight of
Loving My Husband

❦

The noontime mail delivery at my office always caused quite a stir. Seven women would comb the hundreds of envelopes we received until the "prize" was found—my daily letter from C. J. As the only single woman, my long-distance courtship was of great interest to the other six women. I was living in Florida, and C. J. was in Washington, D.C.; so in those days prior to e-mail and cell phones, our relationship was conducted through the U.S. mail.

These women enjoyed the vicarious excitement of our romance, but a knowing laughter would erupt when they talked about the future. "Just wait," they would tell me. "He's 'Mr. Wonderful' now, but that will all change when you get married."

I would always protest that cynical view, but for the ten months of our courtship and engagement, my coworkers never wavered. They unanimously agreed that the fairy tale would end shortly after our honeymoon.

It's sad, but all too often it's true.

We frequently observe women during courtship and maybe even into the first year of marriage who appear to be "madly in love." However, when we interact with these same women several years later, the passion and delight seem strangely absent. Their husbands are no longer "Mr. Wonderful." What happened? Why is there no longer any thrill and excitement? Is this inevitable?

No, it's not meant to be that way! God never intended for wives to abandon their passion and delight for their husbands. In fact, He has in mind quite the opposite. Echoing through the corridors of time come the inspired words from Titus 2:4: "So train the young women to love their husbands."

WHAT IS LOVE?

In the Broadway musical *Fiddler on the Roof*, the main character, Tevye, asks his wife, Golde, "Do you love me?"

In response she reminds him that for twenty-five years she's washed his clothes, cooked his meals, cleaned his house, given him children, and milked his cow. She continues: "For twenty-five years I've lived with him, fought with him, starved with him; twenty-five years my bed is his; *if that's not love, what is?*"[1] (emphasis mine).

That's a good question! What is love? More importantly, what does it mean in Titus 2 when it says we are to love our husbands? The definition couldn't be more different from Golde's!

The form of Greek in which the New Testament was written employs at least five words to distinguish various kinds of love. The word for love used in Titus 2:4 is *phileo*. This word describes the love between very close friends. It is a tender, affectionate, passionate kind of love. It emphasizes enjoyment and respect in a relationship.

LAST TUESDAY

Sad to say, I have been guilty of neglecting this *phileo* kind of love on numerous occasions. I often become so preoccupied with the duties and responsibilities of my marriage that I fail to nurture tenderness and passion in my relationship with my husband. I get so busy *serving* him that I overlook *enjoying* him. For an example, I need only to recall the events of this past Tuesday.

By the time my family stirred from their beds that morning, I had already been awake for several hours. Guests were arriving from out of town for the day, and I was busy cleaning the house. Absorbed in my preparations, I gave C. J. a brief but distracted kiss as he left for work. When he called several hours later to inquire how I was doing,

I kept my answers short. Many tasks still needed my attention, and I certainly didn't have time to ask how his day was going!

After our guests arrived, I took them to lunch. In between driving them around town, I managed to drop C. J.'s pants off at the cleaners, make a deposit at the bank, and fill up the car with gas. I did stop by C. J.'s office, but only to rush in to inform him of my schedule for the remainder of the afternoon. I left so quickly that he barely had time to give me a hug!

I finally returned home from taking our guests to the airport around eight o'clock that evening. After chatting with my children about the events of their day, I headed for bed.

It was some time later before I realized that I had once again failed to love my husband with a tender and passionate love. I had been remiss in expressing physical affection. I had ignored opportunities to communicate care and encouragement. I certainly was not *enjoying* my husband; I was too busy *serving* him!

PHILEO VERSUS AGAPE

In light of my tendency to neglect this tender love, I find it interesting that Paul chose *phileo* rather than *agape* to describe the kind of love we are to have for our husbands.

The Greek word *agape* refers to a self-sacrificing love. It's a love that gives to others even if nothing is given back. It's the love we are urged to pursue in the great love passage of 1 Corinthians 13, so often read at weddings.

Yet Paul didn't use *agape* in describing the love we are to cultivate for our husbands. He chose *phileo*. In fact, in commands specifically related to wives, *agape* is never used. Now this does not mean we have been exempted from needing to extend this kind of love. The second greatest commandment requires each of us to love our neighbor as ourselves (Mark 12:31). Since our husbands are our closest neighbors, we can be sure that we are to love them with a sacrificial love.

Husbands, in contrast, *are* specifically commanded to love their wives with an *agape* kind of love. We see this in Ephesians 5:25, where husbands are told to love their wives "as Christ loved the church and gave himself up for her."

I believe that Scripture's specific commands to husbands and wives regarding their duties in marriage attest to our respective weaknesses. Men may be weaker in showing sacrificial love and are therefore exhorted to undertake it. But I believe women are generally weaker in exhibiting an affectionate love—thus the instructions given to us in Titus 2.

In fact, women will often continue to sacrifice and serve their husbands even if all tender feelings for them have subsided. Author Douglas Wilson makes this observation: "Women are fully capable of loving a man, and sacrificing for him, while believing the entire time that he is a true and unvarnished jerk. Women are good at this kind of love."[2]

I have met women like that! They obviously do not respect their husbands. They certainly do not have tender feelings for them. Yet that does not hinder these women from continuing to wash their husbands' clothes, cook their meals, and clean the house for them.

However, Scripture's mandate to love our husbands involves far more than merely doing household chores. We are required to love them with nothing less than a passionate, tender, affectionate kind of love!

NO CONTINGENCY CLAUSE

When my husband and I purchased our home, the contract we signed contained a contingency clause. This carefully worded paragraph ensured our release from the conditions of the contract if we were unable to sell our previous home within a set period of time.

However, this command to *phileo* does not include a contingency clause! This verse does not say, "Have the older women teach the young women how to love their husbands—*if* they have godly character or *if* they are deserving of this kind of love or *if* they change." We are to love our husbands with a tender, affectionate love regardless of their response. There are no qualifications added to this command. It's an unconditional love.

Maybe there is someone reading this who is asking: "What if I no longer have feelings for my husband? What if I have fallen in love with someone else? Do I have to stay in this marriage if I am not in love anymore?"

If your love for your husband has faded, the question is not: "Should I stay in this marriage?" According to God's Word, the question you *should* be asking is: "How can I, as a wife, bring honor to the gospel?"

And I think we know the answer: We *must* love our husbands. As we learned in chapter 1, this kind of love commends the gospel. If we no longer have tender feelings for our husbands, we must seek God's help to learn how to love them again. First John 4:19 says that we can love our husbands because God first loved us. As we submit to God's command, He will show us how to love, and He will make it possible.

THE LORD OF LOVE

Sally's husband has been looking at pornography on the Internet, *again*. Mary's husband has ceased to show her any physical affection. Christine's husband works long hours and spends most of his free time in front of the television or playing computer games. Anne's husband is not a Christian and has been antagonistic toward her church and Christian friends.

I know all these women. These are not their real names, but their circumstances are very real—and break my heart. I ache for them and the trials they endure. Their seemingly senseless situations pose the question: "How can God expect these women to love their husbands with an affectionate love?"

For the answer, we must view such circumstances in light of the cross, where God the Father sacrificed His only Son. This event did not seem to make sense either. But out of Christ's unspeakable suffering, God, in His perfect wisdom, provided salvation for mankind. If He has purchased our salvation through the suffering and sacrifice of His Son, can we not trust that He is working good in the midst of *our* suffering (Rom. 8:28)?

If you are in an exceptionally trying situation with your husband, I encourage you to pour out your heart to the Lord of love. He knows, He sees, and He hears; and though your tears may be lost on your husband, they are not lost on your heavenly Father. He is the compassionate Lord who urges us to draw near to Him so "that we may receive mercy and find grace to help in time of need" (Heb. 4:16).

Although you may not understand, you can be sure that your marriage has God's loving inscription upon it. God's unerring wisdom has ordained your relationship with your husband—for your good and for

Christ's glory. Look to God for strength to endure, for the Lord promises that He will husband you (Isa. 54:5-6). God will renew your strength so that you will not grow weary in cultivating a tender love for your husband.

Furthermore, you do not know what the Lord has planned for your future. Your tender love for your husband could be the means God uses to soften his heart toward you and toward Himself. I have seen this happen in many marriages.

Now with this encouragement, I also must add an important qualification. I am not saying that a wife is required to remain in a marriage where the biblical exceptions for divorce apply (Matt. 5:32 and 19:9). Nor am I saying that a wife should remain with a physically abusive husband.

For those of you who may be in a situation such as this, I would appeal to you to seek guidance and counsel from your pastor and, where necessary, protection from the authorities. But even then may I remind you that our God is a redeemer? No matter how trying and difficult your circumstances may be, He will help you to reflect the love of Jesus.

THE SCHOOL OF LOVE

Our culture uses the phrase "falling in love" as if some irresistible force overpowers us, and we have no choice but to surrender. But that is misleading and unhelpful.

Loving our husbands with a tender and passionate love is not something that happens automatically in our marriage. Ever since Adam and Eve took that fatal bite of forbidden fruit, our natural human inclination has shifted toward sin. Therefore, we are not naturally prone to love. We are not naturally inclined to be passionate and respectful toward our husbands. In fact, if we do what comes naturally, it will be wrong most of the time!

Rather, we must *learn* how to adopt this kind of love. We see this principle implied in our text. If Paul exhorted Titus to have the older women *teach* the young women how to love their husbands, we can assume this love is not something that happens spontaneously. Loving our husbands—as biblically defined—is a learned response through the grace of God. The good news is that God is eager to teach us this love.

WHERE DID ALL THE LOVE GO?

During my courtship with C. J., he had multiple speaking engage-ments in the local central Florida area. We were both desperate to be together; so as much as possible I would accompany him to these meetings. Before long I began to notice an unusual pattern: Mealtime would come and go, and C. J., preoccupied with ministering to peo-ple, would completely forget to eat. What's more, it didn't occur to him that I might be hungry! However, I didn't mind all that much. I so enjoyed his company that I was easily able to ignore my hunger pangs.

Then we got married. We traveled often during our first year of marriage, and, not surprisingly, eating continued to remain a low pri-ority for C. J. But now I began to grow resentful whenever we missed a meal. *He's not thinking about me. He's more concerned about his min-istry than he is about my needs.* As these thoughts simmered, the lov-ing feelings I felt for my husband turned to vengeful feelings, and these vengeful feelings led to angry reactions.

So where did all my love go?

The answer is very simple: Sin destroyed my tender love.

C. J. hadn't changed. He wasn't behaving any differently than before we were married. He certainly didn't have evil motives—not that this would have justified my anger. But instead of being patient with him as he learned to care for a wife, I began to respond with bit-terness and resentment. Consequently, my tender feelings evaporated.

If we find that our affection for our husband is waning or has subsided altogether, then we do not need to look any further than our own hearts. Where sin is present, warm affection dissipates. Anger, bitterness, criticism, pride, selfishness, fear, laziness—all vig-orously oppose tender love. This love cannot survive in a heart that harbors sin.

KEEP YOUR HEART!

King Solomon, who after the Lord Himself holds the distinction of being the wisest man who ever lived, said, "Keep your heart with all vigilance" (Prov. 4:23). In order to cultivate and maintain a tender love for our husbands, we must guard our hearts against sin.

Our emotions are a warning system God graciously gave us to attract attention to the sin in our hearts. When we're not experiencing loving feelings toward our husbands, that's an alarm going off: ding, ding, ding. There may be sin that needs attention!

I keep one of Jonathan Edwards's resolutions in the front of my devotional notebook and seek to make it my personal resolution. He said, "Resolved, whenever my feelings begin to appear in the least out of order, when I am conscious of the least uneasiness within, or the least irregularity without, I will then subject myself to the strictest examination."[3]

Whenever our "sin alarm" (unloving feelings) goes off, we must examine our hearts and repent of any sin we find there. This is how we maintain a tender love toward our husbands.

Now all this talk about sin may sound harsh, but this truth is the key to freedom and change. When we agree with the diagnosis of Scripture that we have a sinful heart (Rom. 3:23), we can also receive the remedy—the forgiveness of Christ and His power to change.

TEN THOUSAND FAULTS

Like a pebble tossed into a pool of water, awareness of our sinfulness generates a marvelous ripple effect in our marriage. Here's how it works: The more we understand the sin in our hearts, the more we appreciate the patience and mercy of God; and this, in turn, produces an attitude of humility and mercy toward our husbands!

My husband's historical hero Charles Spurgeon once said:

He who grows in grace remembers that he is but dust, and he therefore does not expect his fellow Christians to be anything more. He overlooks ten thousand of their faults, because he knows his God overlooks twenty thousand in his own case. He does not expect perfection in the creature, and, therefore, he is not disappointed when he does not find it.[4]

When we see our husbands as sinners like ourselves—sinners in need of God's grace and mercy—it strips away any intolerant, critical, or demanding attitude we may be tempted to have. Every husband has areas where he needs to change and grow, but so do we!

This doesn't mean we excuse or ignore our husbands' sins. But attentiveness to our *own* sin will create an attitude of humility that is essential when we need to correct our husbands. We must first repent from our own sin before we confront their sin. As it says in Matthew 7:5, when we take the log of sin out of our own eyes, then we will see clearly to take the speck out of our brothers' (or in this case, our husbands') eyes.

Although we both are sinners, God is using our marriage to help us grow in godliness. In fact, our husbands' particular sins, unique weaknesses, and even their idiosyncrasies are tailor-made for us. Likewise, our sins and weaknesses are custom-designed for them. Both husbands and wives will become more Christlike by having to deal with each other's sins and deficiencies.

We must settle this issue in our hearts. We married a sinner, and so did they. But this is the hope for our marriage: God forgives sinners and helps us grow to be like Him.

If you are single, I would encourage you to study these truths now. They will serve you as you interact with single men, encourage your married friends, and prepare for your future—should God call you to marriage. Humility borne of the awareness of our sinful tendencies is an essential character quality in mature Christians. As single women you should cultivate this humility and look for it in any man who might pursue you for marriage.

TENDER THOUGHTS

Your husband comes home from work, heads to the nearest comfy chair, and pulls the newspaper up in front of his face. What sort of thoughts run through your mind? Are they kind thoughts? Loving thoughts? Or thoughts you dare not reveal?

We frequently face situations where we are tempted to think harsh and critical thoughts. Sometimes as wives we are more inclined to concentrate on what our husbands are doing wrong than what they are doing right. We are more aware of their deficiencies than areas where they excel. But if we submit to these temptations, they will only lead to the demise of warm affection.

Rather, we must choose to focus on our husbands' many commendable qualities. As we do this, we will be amazed. We'll start to discover more and more good qualities that we were failing to see because we were blinded by our critical thoughts.

In her book *Love Has a Price Tag*, Elisabeth Elliot includes some very good counsel from her husband for wives:

> A wife, if she is very generous, may allow that her husband lives up to perhaps eighty percent of her expectations. There is always the other twenty percent that she would like to change, and she may chip away at it for the whole of their married life without reducing it by very much. She may, on the other hand, simply decide to enjoy the eighty percent, and both of them will be happy.[5]

The apostle Paul understood the influence of people's thoughts on their feelings and behavior. He exhorted the Philippians in this way: "Finally, brothers, whatever is true, whatever is honorable, whatever is just, whatever is pure, whatever is lovely, whatever is commendable, if there is any excellence, if there is anything worthy of praise, think about these things" (Phil. 4:8). If we make it our aim to think these kinds of thoughts about our husbands, we will experience tender feelings for them. As Shirley Rice writes:

> Are you in love with your husband? Not, Do you love him? I know you do. He has been around a long time, and you're used to him. He is the father of your children. But are you in love with him? How long has it been since your heart really squeezed when you looked at him? . . . Why is it you have forgotten the things that attracted you to him at first? . . . Your husband needs to be told that you love him, that he is attractive to you. By the grace of God, I want you to start changing your thought pattern. Tomorrow morning, get your eyes off the toaster or the baby bottles long enough to LOOK at him. Don't you see the way his coat fits his shoulders? Look at his hands. Do you remember when just to look at his strong hands made your heart lift? Well, LOOK at him and remember. Then loose your tongue and tell him you love him. Will you ask the Lord to give you a sentimental, romantic, physical, in-love kind of love for your husband? He will do this.[6]

Let's heed Shirley's advice: If we have forgotten the things that first attracted us to our husbands, *let's change our thought pattern* and start to remember them.

Now I am not just promoting the helpful counsel of a wise woman here. But isn't her recommendation to wives in keeping with the counsel of holy Scripture: "Whatever is true, whatever is honorable, whatever is just, whatever is pure, whatever is lovely, whatever is commendable, if there is any excellence, if there is anything worthy of praise, think about these things"? I dare say it is.

Let's humbly ask our heavenly Father to help us change our thought patterns and then watch what He will do. As we begin to replace sinful thoughts with biblical thinking, the Lord will ignite passionate feelings for our husbands once again.

TENDER BEHAVIOR

Tender thoughts are only the beginning! As Linda Dillow says, "Now that you know your husband's admirable qualities, why keep them to yourself? It's good to admire your husband secretly, but how much better to admire him actively!"[7] We can admire our husbands actively by *prizing* them, *cherishing* them, and *enjoying* them.

Prize Him

Michelle poured her life and energy into her two small children. However, the demands and joys of motherhood crowded out her love for her husband. Friendships and service in the church even took precedence over her relationship with Peter. They didn't have any major problems, but their marriage certainly wasn't exciting anymore. Intimate communication and even daily expressions of affection had dwindled. After nine years of marriage, their relationship more closely resembled an amiable business partnership. Michelle was so busy raising her daughters, she didn't even notice.

Michelle had ceased to "prize" her husband. There was a time when Peter was the most important person in her life, but over time her children and friends had become more significant. However, according to Scripture, these are faulty priorities.

The Bible makes it very clear that, after our relationship with God, our relationship with our husband is to be our highest priority. In the creation account of the book of Genesis, we discover that woman was created to be her husband's helper (Gen. 2:18). The same is restated in the New Testament: "For man was not made from woman, but woman from man. Neither was man created for woman, but woman for man" (1 Cor. 11:8-9). Then in our Titus 2 passage we see that the list of instructions for the younger women begins and ends with their relationship to their husbands.

Notice from the aforementioned verses that we were created to be our husband's helper, not our children's mother. Certainly we are to love, care for, and nurture our children (we will talk more about this in the next chapter), but this love is to flow out of a lifestyle that is first and foremost committed to helping our husbands. Our husbands should always remain first in our hearts and in our care.

In fact, one of the most loving things we can do for our children is to prize our husbands. It provides a wonderful security in their lives, and it presents a biblical model for them and their future marriages. We want our daughters to prize their future husbands; and for our sons, we want them to find wives who will prize them.

Michelle was unaware that she was putting her children before her husband until several faithful friends from church brought it to her attention. "It was like waking up," she said. "I was blind to it." Michelle immediately began to make changes. She started by praying each day that God would give her greater love for Peter. But she didn't stop there. She began to express affection in creative ways—through cards and letters. She took time to think about things that would bless Peter. She sought his opinion first instead of going to her friends. In short, she made her relationship with her husband her highest priority!

Her actions had a tangible effect. As a couple they began to pursue interests and activities that *didn't* involve the children. "Things went so well," Peter said, "that we began to look for more opportunities to steal away together and have fun and enjoy each other." For their anniversary they spent a weekend alone. "The most enjoyable part was simply enjoying one another and our newfound romance. We had a blast!"

Let's heed Scripture's counsel and follow Michelle's example. We should do whatever it takes to let our husbands know that we prize them above all others!

Cherish Him

Remember that we vowed in our wedding ceremony "to love and to *cherish* till death do us part"? Do we even understand what we promised to do? To cherish means to hold dear, to care for tenderly or to nurture, to cling fondly to, or treat as precious.

So how do we make our husbands feel cherished? Who better to ask than husbands? I queried a number of men: "What is one way your wife cherishes you?" Here are some of their answers:

"If I'm sick in bed, my wife prepares tea and meals for me without my asking and waits on me hand and foot. It's as though her world stops so she can take care of me."

"Each time Karin catches my eye in public with a smile and subtle wink, or greets me with a warm embrace upon my arrival home from work, or hangs on my arm when we go out on a date, the message comes through loud and clear: 'I enjoy being with you and want you to know that I love you.'"

"With just a handful of exceptions, Lisa has written me a note in my lunch every single workday for over ten years."

"If I am struggling with a sin, Bonnie will communicate her love for me before bringing correction. Her care for me in those moments is when I feel most cherished because I know she loves me, even at my worst."

"Valori cherishes me by regularly encouraging me in my walk with God and thanking me for pursuing Him with all my heart. This encourages me to persevere, even when I am walking through trials."

"My wife shows me affection through a constant stream of small surprises—showing up at work with my favorite Starbucks drink, making her famous brownies on no special occasion, arranging to borrow a friend's convertible sports car for our anniversary. Not all have been extremely costly, but all have been very meaningful."

"Julie is an astute observer of my life and my needs. She listens carefully whenever I express the smallest desire for something. Along with normal holidays, she will frequently pick up gifts that are relevant, timely, and special to me."

"I am cherished by my wife through her fervent and faithful intercessory prayer for me. Her conviction is that no one can care for me like my heavenly Father."

May these examples spark our own creativity! Let's think of one way that we can cherish our husbands today.

Enjoy Him

Phileo is not a dutiful love; it is to be characterized by joy and delight. We are to find great happiness in our relationship with our husbands. We should prefer their company above all others. We should find genuine pleasure in serving them, and we should take an interest in what they enjoy.

Now taking an interest doesn't necessarily mean that we have to duplicate their enthusiasm or involvement. But the fact that we are even *interested* in what they enjoy will be meaningful to them.

Though there are some areas where I have not done so well at enjoying what my husband enjoys (sports being just one), I *have* come to appreciate one of his favorite pastimes. My husband loves to read. In fact, on our honeymoon he took one whole suitcase filled only with books! Now to his defense, he didn't actually read any of those books. But that gives you a clue as to how much he enjoys this activity. His habit, *no matter what time* we get into bed at night, is to prop himself up and read for at least twenty minutes before going to sleep.

When we were first married, this bedtime habit really irritated me. I would be particularly unhappy with the routine on nights when I was dog-tired but couldn't sleep because the light was still on. However, I came to realize that *I* was the one who needed to adjust. So I chose to join my husband. Now I prop myself up, get *my* book out, and read with him. And guess what? It has become one of our favorite things to do together.

Even if it's not our preference, we should make an effort to enjoy those things that interest our husbands. Who knows? God may surprise us. We may end up actually liking them!

A LOVE THAT LASTS

Our gracious God delights to honor our obedience. As we seek to prize, cherish, and enjoy our husbands, He will freely fill our hearts with love and affection for them. This will happen *regardless* of your circumstances—no matter how long it has been since you have felt or demonstrated affection for your husband, no matter how many times you have tried and failed. God is eager to impart fresh grace to you

His grace provides all that we need to love our husbands. In fact, God *lavishes* us with grace. Charles Spurgeon described God's bountiful provision in this way: "He gives grace abundantly, seasonably, constantly, readily, sovereignly. . . . He generously pours into [our] souls without ceasing, and He always will do so, whatever may occur."[8]

Contrary to the advice of my well-meaning office mates, God gives us grace to cultivate *phileo*—not only during courtship or our first year of marriage but for our entire married lives. So the next time we meet a woman who is getting married, let's tell her about the wonderful grace of God that makes it possible to love her husband more and more with each passing year!

3

The Blessings of Loving My Children

❧

Snaking back and forth through chain-link queues, we saw the same families at every turn. The lines tested the limits of human endurance. In the Florida humidity, everything was sticky with perspiration, spilled soda, and smeared coconut-scented sun block. Sweaty, red-faced children leaned wearily on their parents, who grimaced at the extra body heat. Rising above the amusement park "muzak" were the voices of families on holiday:

"Quit it! Quit touching me. *Mom!* Make her stop touching me!"

"I told you that if we didn't get here earlier, we'd spend all day in lines. But you never listen to me."

"Get over here *this minute!* Did you hear me? Don't make me yell at you one more time, or we'll go home now."

"*No!* I don't want to do that. How come we *never* do what I want to do?"

Marveling at the mass crankiness, C. J. looked at me and asked, "Where are all the families we saw on the cover of the brochure?"

You don't have to go to an amusement park to run across crabby people, however. You can find families like these at any mall or restaurant. To a certain extent, we can all identify with these families. Aren't there days when, if someone were observing inside our homes, they might see an irritated, impatient mother with a pack of whiny children?

Motherhood can be both exhilarating and exasperating. It can present us with a delightful experience one moment and a baffling encounter the next. There are days when we can't imagine doing anything more rewarding. Then we have days when caring for our children feels anything *but* significant. I know. I have been a mother for twenty-seven years. I have three lovely adult daughters and one wonderful ten-year-old son. I can attest to the fact that mothering includes a vast and varying range of experiences that produce inconsistent feelings and conflicting emotions.

However, our perspective of motherhood should not be defined by our diverse experiences and fluctuating emotions. Rather, we must discover God's view and estimation. Our Titus 2 passage exhorts us to love our children—a phrase loaded with meaning for modern mothers. This topic will occupy our attention for the remainder of the chapter.

Even if you don't have children, may I invite you to stick with me? The biblical principles in this chapter will serve you in any relationships you have with children—from your nieces and nephews to the children of your friends. As you model the loving godliness described here, you will win a special place in their hearts.

AN UNCOMMON LOVE

> In the moment my first son was delivered out of my body and into my arms, the world tilted. Miraculous life! How fiercely I loved him, and how urgently I plunged into my new vocation, this career of the heart called motherhood.[1]

Author Katrina Kenison captures the wonder we felt when our newborn was first placed in our arms. What overpowering sensations of love we experienced for that child! We had no need for someone to come alongside and tell us to love our baby. Not at that moment anyway.

But things *do* change. In the days, weeks, and years ahead—as we begin to face the persistent crying of a newborn, the temper tantrums of a two-year-old, the whining of a four-year-old, the disrespect of a ten-year-old, the selfishness of a teenager (or you fill in the blank)—we don't always feel those same tender emotions we experienced in the birthing room at the hospital. We very quickly discover that this affection is not always easy to sustain.

Yet it's in the midst of the trials and challenges of motherhood that the command comes to love our children. Once again the Greek word *phileo* is used to describe the kind of love we are to show. As with our husbands, we are to love our children with a tender, affectionate, and passionate love.

Although many mothers are committed to caring sacrificially for their children, they sometimes neglect to enjoy them. They fulfill the responsibilities of motherhood but overlook the pleasures. I have often erred in this way myself.

Now it is noble to be faithful to the task of serving our children. But Titus 2 calls us to something more (and definitely not less) than a sacrificial and dutiful love. We are to delight in our children!

Let us not forget why. As we discovered in the first chapter, the promotion of the gospel is the impetus behind the commands in Titus 2. The mandate to love our children is no exception. This *phileo* kind of love is appealing to the observant audience of our lives. It stands out in stark contrast to the strife and discord in families all around us and thus draws attention to the transforming effect of the gospel. May this extraordinary call to commend the gospel infuse our hearts with fresh vision and enthusiasm as we seek to love our children!

NO WEEKENDS OFF

"Congratulations, Mrs. Layman," the nurse said to my mom when she brought her first newborn and laid him in her arms. "Your sleeping days are over."

Every mother knows the reality of that congratulatory statement! In the career of motherhood there are no weekends off, no paid vacations, no bonuses or yearly raises, and no quitting time. It is just day-in and day-out giving. There are times when we feel we do not have another ounce of energy left to offer. What we wouldn't do to curl up on the sofa with a good book, enjoy a long, leisurely bubble bath, or simply take a nap. Yet multiple needs still require our attention!

I am convinced that no profession requires harder work or greater sacrifice than motherhood. Stephen and Janet Bly provide us with this job description:

No job on earth takes more physical, mental, social, emotional, and spiritual strength than being a good wife and mother. If a woman is looking for the easy life she might try teaching tennis, cutting diamonds, or joining a roller derby team. There is nothing easy about good mothering. It can be back breaking, heart wrenching and anxiety producing. And that's just the morning.[2]

Because mothering requires constant sacrifice, the temptations to resentment, complaining, and self-pity are always close at hand. But such selfishness will quickly sap the strength of our love for our children.

I will never forget a time when my selfishness robbed me of the joy of caring for my family. My second daughter, Kristin, was ten years old, and we were out on a "date." While our children were growing up, C. J. and I spent special one-on-one times with them each month. It was Kristin's turn that day. We were eating lunch at a restaurant, and I was asking her questions as usual.

"Kristin," I began, "if there was one thing about Mommy that you could change, what would it be?"

"You haven't been smiling very much lately, Mommy," she replied. "You just haven't seemed very happy."

Oh, how those words pierced me! I realized in a moment that motherhood had become a duty instead of a joy. I was so focused on the sacrifices that I had failed to appreciate the daily pleasures of raising my children. This had wiped away my smile.

As mothers, we have a choice. We can either resent the challenges and demands that accompany motherhood and persist in our selfishness, or we can draw from God's grace and receive His help to *cheerfully* lay down our lives for our children.

Let's choose the latter.

If we do, we are choosing biblical greatness. As Jesus said in Matthew 20:26: "Whoever would be *great* among you must be your servant" (emphasis mine).

The world may not applaud us for wiping runny noses, driving in carpools, or talking with our teenager into the wee hours of the morning. And until they are trained, our children might not thank us either. But as we set aside our own selfish desires and glorify God by joyfully serving our children, we are pursuing true greatness according to the Bible. Let us do so with tenderness, affection, and with a smile!

STRENGTH FOR THE WEARY

But what if you have lost your smile? How do you find renewed joy to sacrificially serve and tenderly love your children? *Our only genuine source of refreshment comes from God.* In Him alone do we acquire fresh strength to carry out this enormous task of mothering.

So may I encourage you to seize some time alone to meet with God? This should already be our daily practice, but in seasons of weariness, there is tremendous benefit in withdrawing for a more lengthy time to pray and read God's Word.

Now some of you mothers with little ones might be asking, "How is 'alone time' possible? I cannot even go to the bathroom by myself, much less consider an extended period of solitude!"

Maybe your husband could arrange this time for you, or possibly you could trade off with another mom. Whatever it takes, it's worth the effort to make it happen!

Taking time to meet with God is a practice modeled for us by Jesus Himself. We read in Luke 5 that multitudes were coming to Him with their needs: "Crowds of people came to hear him and to be healed of their sicknesses. *But Jesus often withdrew to lonely places and prayed*" (vv. 15-16, NIV, emphasis mine).

Doesn't this sound like a description of motherhood—everyone coming to Mom with needs? Yet look at what Jesus did. He withdrew to solitary places and prayed.

Now if Jesus needed to withdraw frequently and pray in order to receive His Father's help and strength, do we suppose we need such times any less? So if you are weary, or if your joy and vision for motherhood is waning, take some time this week to be alone with God.

BEWARE OF INDULGENCE

Now before we explore the contours of a tender love, there is an important caution we need to consider. We must not allow our warm affection to degenerate into indulgence. To indulge our children means to allow them to use, do, or have what they want to the detriment of their character.

Do we give in to our three-year-old's demands at the grocery store? Do we supply our eight-year-old with whatever toy or gadget is the latest fad? Or do we allow our teenager to watch movies that undermine biblical values? In our effort to *enjoy* our children, we must never become tolerant of sinful behavior or lenient toward worldly compromise.

Proverbs 22:6 says, "Train up a child in the way he should go; even when he is old he will not depart from it." We have the responsibility, along with our husbands, to train our children. This is no small job! It involves being a godly example, and it requires ongoing teaching and consistent correction. Though a tender love should affect all of our training, it should never impair our authority or hinder our discipline.

Giving In to Selfishness

"Skittles, Mommy," Daniel pleaded as they walked through the grocery store. He then repeated the phrase with a slightly more demanding tone: "Skittles, Mommy."

"No," said Sara for the second time. But Daniel wasn't to be deterred. Fifteen "Skittles, Mommy" later, an exasperated Sara finally relented.

Like my friend Sara, I have given into the whims and wishes of my children—even when I knew it wasn't beneficial for them. I didn't want to endure their inevitable crying or deal with their need for discipline. However, this is laziness and selfishness, and the consequences will negatively affect both our children and us.

I have been sobered by the words of Charles Bridges, first written in 1846: "Far better that [children] should *cry* under healthful correction, than that parents should afterwards *cry* under the bitter fruit to themselves and children, of neglected discipline."[3]

Scripture says the avoidance of discipline is an expression of hate, not love (Prov. 13:24). We certainly do not want to "hate" our children, nor do we want to "cry" later! Therefore, we must not neglect discipline in our pursuit of a *phileo* kind of love.

Giving In to Fear

Now as mothers, we naturally want our children to like us, to approve of us. However, we must never allow this desire for our children's approval to control our mothering.

The Bible calls this "the fear of man" (Prov. 29:25), or in this case, the fear of children. My husband defines this fear as "an excessive sinful concern about what our children think of us, an inordinate desire for our children's approval, or an intense fear of being rejected by our children." Succumbing to the fear of children can lead to indulgence.

If we cave in to our children's sinful demands in order to secure their approval and affection, or if we withhold discipline so as not to risk their displeasure—this is sinful indulgence, not biblical love.

Growing in warm, affectionate love does not conflict with the responsibility to teach and discipline our children. Quite the opposite is true. Tenderness actually softens our children's hearts and wins their affection, which helps them to more readily receive our instruction and correction. This tender love is a key to successful training!

Now that we are mindful of the dangers of indulgence, let's turn our attention toward developing a warm and tender love.

TENDER THOUGHTS

I knew my friend was just trying to be helpful, but as she talked, anxiety rose in my heart. "You know," she said, "I recently read that a newborn requires thirty to forty hours a week of care. . . ."

It was only a matter of days before I was due to deliver our fourth child, our son Chad. Because it had been almost twelve years since the birth of my last baby, I was already apprehensive about the adjustments his arrival would bring. My friend certainly wasn't helping matters!

Thirty to forty hours! Where am I going to find that kind of time? How will I be able to care for this child adequately in addition to everything else? The more I thought about it, the more anxiety I felt. I lay awake at night, trying to calculate how I could squeeze the extra hours into my already bulging schedule. It seemed an impossible feat.

Then I remembered Psalm 127: "Behold, children are a heritage from the LORD, the fruit of the womb a reward. Like arrows in the hand of a warrior are the children of one's youth. Blessed is the man who fills his quiver with them!" (vv. 3-5).

As I read those words, I realized how sinful my outlook had become. I had been viewing this baby as "a forty-hour work week." But God wanted me to think of him as a reward.

That is exactly what Chad was! Instead of the major challenge I had envisioned, his arrival brought nothing but pure joy to our family. Like any newborn, Chad did require many hours of care. However, now that I had gained a biblical perspective, the responsibility was a delight and not a burden.

What words or images come to your mind when you think about your children? Are you inclined like I was to think: *work, responsibility, sacrifice, burden, more work?*

Look at the words the psalmist used to describe children: *heritage, fruit, reward, arrows.* Then he followed with this exclamation: "Blessed is the man who fills his quiver with them!"

Our speech and actions are shaped by our thoughts. Therefore, we must make every effort to think Psalm 127 kinds of thoughts about our children. Thinking of them as a heritage, a reward, and a blessing will alter our attitude and provide the fertile soil for our tender love to grow.

TENDER BEHAVIOR

On his long-running television show *House Party*, the host Art Linkletter interviewed thousands of children. He included many of these conversations in a book entitled *Kids Say the Darndest Things.* Kids *do* say funny things, and at times they also say insightful things.

With that in mind, I decided to conduct some interviews of my own. I asked a number of young people how they knew that their moms loved them. The following is a sampling of their responses:

"She consistently makes wonderful meals without complaint." Jimmy

"My mom is always asking, 'Do you know I love you? Do you know I'm for you? Do you know I'm your biggest fan?'" Kelley

"She writes me notes and letters. She is always encouraging me." Andrew

"I don't think I've gone a day in my life without my mom telling me she is praying for me." Israel

"Whenever I wake up in the morning, go to bed at night, or come home from somewhere, she hugs me and says that she loves me. This is very securing. I love it a lot." Brittany

"My mom plays chess and checkers with me." Matt

"When I come home from somewhere and she knows I am going to be very tired, she asks what food she can make for me." Evan

"My mom loves to have my friends over. She likes taking us out and doing things with us. She loves my friends. They are her friends too." Kristin

"When I was little and couldn't sleep, my mom would rock me and sing songs to me. Now at bedtime she always comes into my room for five or ten minutes and asks me about my day." Bryce

"My mom is never too busy to talk to me. She tells me that she would rather be at home with me than doing anything else." Erin

"Every day before I go to school, my mom asks how she can pray for me. Then when I come home, she tells me what she prayed during the day." Jimmy

"She comes to all of my games. I can always hear her cheering for me. She's my #1 fan." Stephen

"My mom takes me out one time a month. We go to lunch and just talk." Kristin

"When it is cold outside and I have to drive to school, my mom turns my car facing out of the driveway and starts the heater so it is warm by the time I'm ready to leave." Melanie

"When my brothers and I were little, she would always fix hot chocolate with marshmallows for us when it was cold." Chris

"My mom packs a lunch for me every day and puts in a note that says 'I love you' or has Scripture on it." Brian

"She reads me books at night." Brielle

What is remarkable to me about these children's comments is how simple these acts of love are. Tender love is not complicated! It doesn't require a large bank account or creative genius. Rather, this love consists of seemingly insignificant activities like cooking, singing, reading, or talking. It includes faithful prayer and encouragement or small gestures of kindness.

Chances are, you may already be doing many of these things. So be encouraged—they *are* meaningful to your children! And if you realize there are ways you need to grow in expressing tender love, may these children's observations provide you with fresh inspiration and ideas.

NUMBER OUR DAYS

Let's seize the opportunity we have *right now* to love our children with a *phileo* kind of love! Though it is easy to become distracted by the constant demands of motherhood, we must not lose sight of this fact: *Our children are only young for a very brief time.*

When my girls were little, it wasn't always easy for me to wake up for those 2:00 A.M. feedings. Loneliness sometimes crept in when I missed an activity in order to put them to bed on time. I was eager to get them potty-trained and be done with the dirty diaper routine. Some days it felt as if that season would never end.

But frequently on trips to the grocery store a grandmother would stop to admire my little ones and leave me with this admonition: "Honey, enjoy them now because they grow up so quickly."

How right those women were!

I was keenly aware of the fleetingness of childhood when my son Chad was born. At the time of his birth, Nicole was sixteen, Kristin was fifteen, and Janelle was eleven. By now experience had taught me to treasure each moment, for I knew he wouldn't stay small very long.

The challenges of mothering seemed altogether insignificant this time around. Middle-of-the-night feedings weren't drudgery. I hardly gave a moment's thought to missing an activity. I certainly wasn't in a hurry to potty-train my son. In fact, much to the chagrin of my three daughters, I did not tend to that task until he was almost four years old. (By that time, it only took one day to train him!)

Moms, you may be up to your earlobes with babies and dirty diapers. Or you may be spending half your life in the car, driving your children to and from numerous activities. In whatever stage of motherhood you find yourself, may I remind you of something? It won't last for very long!

Katrina Kenison observes how swiftly children grow up:

> Just when I figure out how to mother a kindergartner, it seems, I have a first-grader standing before me instead. I have just learned how to love and live with a nine-year-old when the nine-year-old vanishes, leaving a preadolescent in his place. They don't stay still long enough for me to have my fill of them ever, at any stage. "Stop!" I want to shout. "Let's just do it this way for a while, let's stay right here." But the movement is inexorable—up and out, away, into the future.[4]

In Psalm 90 Moses depicted the reality of the brevity of life. He compared our lives to a watch in the night, a dream, grass that flourishes and then fades—all brief and fleeting images. Then he prayed this way: "So teach us to number our days" (v. 12).

Have you numbered your days lately? If we pause to count the remaining days we have with our children, we will realize how few there are. This awareness will help to safeguard us from neglecting a tender love.

As I once heard someone say: "It's only a snap of the finger from diapers to tuxedos and wedding gowns." How well I know this to be true. My three daughters are already married. It doesn't seem that long ago when I cradled them in my arms for the very first time.

OUR HIGHEST OBJECTIVE

What is the ultimate purpose of a *phileo* kind of love? It is nothing less than the salvation of our children's souls. This is the chief end of mothering. Our goal is not that our children be happy, fulfilled, and successful. Granted, we may desire these things for them. But our highest objective should be that our children would repent from their sins, put their trust in Jesus Christ, and reflect the gospel to the world around them.

J. C. Ryle offered the following admonition:

> This is the thought that should be uppermost on your mind in all you do for your children. In every step you take about them, in every plan, and scheme, and arrangement that concerns them, do not leave out that mighty question, *"How will this affect their souls?"*

. . . the chief end of [their lives] is the salvation of [their] soul[s].[5]

While the salvation of our children is our highest aim, our tender love is not sufficient for this task. Only the Holy Spirit is able to reveal the truth of the gospel. However, our tender love can be an instrument in God's hands. I am convinced that no one has more potential to influence our children to receive and reflect the gospel than we do as mothers. John Angell James in *Female Piety* illustrated this very point:

> At a pastoral conference, held not long since, at which about one hundred and twenty American clergymen, united in the bonds of a common faith, were assembled, each was invited to state the human instrumentality to which, under the Divine blessing, he attributed a change of heart. How many of these, think you, gave the honour of it to their mother? Of one hundred and twenty, above one hundred! Here then are facts, which are only selected from myriads of others, to prove a mother's power, and to demonstrate at the same time her responsibility. [6]

What greater privilege could we possibly have in all the world than to lead our children to the Lord? Let us not for one moment underestimate the power of a tender love!

GRAVE RESPONSIBILITY, GREATER GRACE

No one needs to remind us that it is an enormous responsibility to be a mother. How well we know it! One woman expresses it this way:

> I seldom feel like much of an adventurer—standing in this kitchen, pouring cereal into bowls, refilling them, handing out paper towels when the inevitable cry comes: "Uh oh. I spilled." But sometimes at night the thought will strike me: There are three small people here, breathing sweetly in their beds, whose lives are for the moment in our hands. I might as well be at the controls of a moon shot, the mission is so grave and vast.[7]

Though the mission is grave and vast, God's grace is greater. He kindly reminds us in His Word: "My grace is sufficient for you, for my power is made perfect in weakness" (2 Cor. 12:9).

So if today you missed opportunities to show a tender love, or if you neglected to pray for your children, or if you were impatient with them, and even if you lost your smile and feel like a complete failure as a mother—take heart!

God's grace *is* sufficient for you. Look to the cross where Christ died. There He purchased forgiveness for our sins and power to grow in godliness. Not one of us is equal to this task of mothering, but He will help us in our weakness. God will provide all the grace we need to love our children tenderly.

The Safety of Self-Control

Recently someone told me about a talk show on which family members challenged their loved ones to give up something they felt they couldn't live without—for one entire week.

A sister dared her twin to relinquish her cell phone. A daughter appealed to her mom to stop spending all her time on the Internet, and one mother implored her teenage daughter to cease her daily consumption of cupcakes.

Each relative issuing the challenge was provided with a video camera to follow the person's daily activities. One by one, the videotape revealed that these individuals couldn't resist temptation. None of them were able to completely abandon their most prized activity, not even with the added pressure of a television audience!

And don't we all have our own examples of failure and defeat to tell? Have you ever set goals for yourself in January and by February forgotten what they were? Have you ever eaten that second piece of chocolate cake—all the while ignoring your guilty conscience? Or have you lashed out in anger at your child only moments after repenting from your last outburst?

I have. And, sad to say, I could give plenty of other examples.

Fortunately, the writer of Romans could relate. Listen to Paul's lament: "I have the desire to do what is right, but not the ability to carry it out. For I do not do the good I want, but the evil I do not want is what I keep on doing" (Rom. 7:18-19). I know of no words that so succinctly capture our struggle with sin. Therefore, how do we deal with this formidable force so as not to live a life dominated by failure?

We have the answer in our Titus 2 passage. It is the third quality on the Titus 2 list—the virtue of self-control. Self-control is what we need in order to say no to sinful desires, what we need to follow through on godly desires. Self-control will enable us to *meet* those goals, *decline* that chocolate cake, and *resist* the temptation to lash out at our child.

OH NO—NOT SELF-CONTROL!

Even as I write *that word*, I think I'm hearing a collective groan. Just the mention of self-control is enough to cause some of you to look around for other reading material! It conjures up words like *drudgery, discipline, discouragement,* and even *despair.* We think of this quality as the antithesis of all that we enjoy in life. We may even feel that we have attempted self-control hundreds of times, but it just doesn't work.

Furthermore, self-control is not a popular topic today. The latest women's magazines certainly aren't advertising "The Five Secrets of Self-Control." Even in the church, this quality is unfortunately often neglected in favor of other more palatable topics. But we as Christians need to reexamine this virtue from a biblical perspective.

Self-control is so important that the apostle Paul required it, directly or by inference, of every group of Christians he addressed in the Titus 2 chapter. The emphasis placed on this virtue reveals how essential self-control is if we are to effectively commend the gospel. We cannot afford to ignore it!

Therefore, if Scripture *requires* self-control from every Christian, it is obviously *attainable* by every Christian. This truth should revolutionize our understanding of self-control. For whenever God gives a command, He also provides the grace to obey it.

A BETTER STRENGTH

We're all too familiar with them—those diet advertisements that claim *their plan* is the salvation of women everywhere. A slim and stylish female is pictured next to an image of herself 100 pounds ago. (Of course, in the "before" picture she is dressed in sweats and wearing no makeup.) She tells her tale—how she tried every diet program available, without success—*until now*. And just look at her! You too can achieve her attractive figure. All you have to do is call the number at the bottom of the screen.

If only self-control were as easy as dialing an 800 number. But it's not!

Self-control doesn't just happen. We can't adopt the indifferent attitude "let go and let God" and expect magically to become self-controlled. Self-control requires effort. However, development of this quality is not solely dependent upon us. We cannot acquire this virtue by our own strength. It is only as we cooperate with the power of the Holy Spirit that we will achieve self-control. Our growth will take place as it did with Paul who said, "For this I toil, struggling with all his energy that he powerfully works within me" (Col. 1:29). Notice that Paul *did* toil and struggle, but his effort was initiated and sustained by the Holy Spirit.

We are to work hard at taking control of our lives, but our success is only ensured as we participate with the Holy Spirit. As Charles Bridges has written:

> Man may talk of self-control, as if the reins were in his own hands. But he who has been "born of the Spirit," and taught "to know the plague of his own heart," is made to feel that effective self-control is divine grace, not his own native power. . . . Have not repeated defeats taught us the need of calling in better strength than our own?[1]

The good news is that Christ is more than willing to grant us His "better strength." In fact, Scripture says that He is always present to help us in our time of need. He delights to bring glory to His name by enabling us to overcome patterns of sin. So with fresh faith let's revisit the biblical teaching of self-control.

A PROTECTIVE WALL

In ancient times, a city without walls was inconceivable. The walls were its main defense, and without them a city was easy prey to its enemies. Any neighboring country could attack the city at will, guaranteeing suffering for the whole community. Wild animals could threaten their small children and plunder their gardens. Only strong walls could protect them from vulnerability to attack.

God's Word likens self-control to walls, or rather it informs us that *not* having self-control is like *not* having walls. We read in Proverbs 25:28: "A man without self-control is like a city broken into and left without walls."

At the time Solomon wrote his proverbs, many Hebrew cities were surrounded by both an outer wall, more than four feet thick, and an inner wall that was three feet thick. When we understand the image Solomon had in mind, we see more clearly our need for self-control and the protection it secures.

Self-control is our wall of defense against the enemies of our soul. Indeed we are up against some powerful enemies. Just as Allied soldiers in World War II fought in the European *and* Pacific Theaters of battle, we too face conflict on various fronts. We have the Worldly Theater, the Devil's Theater, and—most insidious of all—the Inner Theater.

Scripture warns us that the world hates us (John 15:19), the enemy seeks to devour us (1 Pet. 5:8), and our sinful desires wage war against our souls (1 Pet. 2:11). These desires are deceitful (Eph. 4:22); they drag us away and entice us into sin (James 1:14).

As Jerry Bridges observes: "What makes these sinful desires so dangerous is that they dwell within our own heart. External temptations would not be nearly so dangerous were it not for the fact that they find this ally of desire right within our own breast."[2]

We are in a fierce battle—confronting sin from within and temptations from without. But God provides a means of protection in this war. He wants to encircle us with a wall that can withstand the onslaughts on all three fronts. That wall is self-control.

GETTING REAL ABOUT WHAT WE ENJOY

The first step in constructing this wall of self-control is to acknowledge one simple yet hideous fact about ourselves: We like to sin! This may not be easy to concede, but it's true.

When we hit the snooze button for the third time, it's because we *like* to sleep. When we reply to our husbands with a cruel remark, it's because we *want* to inflict hurt. When we buy that new outfit even though we can't afford it, it's because we *covet* new clothes. Admitting to these ungodly delights is the starting point in our quest for self-control.

God's Word confronts us with the harsh reality of the gratification we derive from our sin. Though it acknowledges sin's pleasure, it also cautions us that this pleasure is short-lived (Heb. 11:25). Our enjoyment of sin doesn't last very long.

So what happens after the euphoria dissipates? I think we all know the answer to that question. Sin always leads to death (Rom. 6:15-23). Sin delivers negative consequences not only in our own lives, but also in our relationships with others.

Think of the illustrations we've just considered. We revel in the luxury of extra sleep, but we spend the rest of the day frantically trying to make up for lost time. We exult in the brief moment of victory over our husbands, but we later regret the rift we've created in our marriage. Or we like showing off that new outfit, but we face the costly consequences when the bill arrives.

We desperately need the grace of self-control to avoid sin's destructive cycles. When we recognize self-control as the virtue that spares us from sin's negative consequences, we will welcome it eagerly as our friend.

In the remainder of this chapter we will focus on self-control as it relates to our appetites, our thoughts and feelings, and our behavior. However, let me insert a caution before we embark on this study: Please don't make an exhaustive list of every area where change is needed! That is only a set-up for defeat. But let me encourage you to prayerfully consider one or two areas for application and then devote yourself specifically to these in the coming weeks.

OUR APPETITES

If you have read the book of Romans recently, you know that Paul used the first eleven chapters to unfurl the mercies of God. Then, with God's mercy in view, Paul issued the following plea in the first verse of chapter twelve: "I appeal to you therefore, brothers, by the mercies of God, to present your bodies as a living sacrifice, holy and acceptable to God, which is your spiritual worship."

The only appropriate response to the mercies of God is to yield ourselves fully to Him—starting with our bodies—and grow into a new life of holiness. Elisabeth Elliot comments on this verse:

> More spiritual failure is due, I believe, to this cause than to any other: the failure to recognize this living body as having anything to do with worship or holy sacrifice. This body is, quite simply, the starting place. Failure here is failure everywhere else. . . .
>
> We cannot give our hearts to God and keep our bodies for ourselves.[3]

Undisciplined use of our bodies will hinder our service to God. For example, the amount of sleep we get—whether too much or too little—can interfere with our daily communion with God and ability to care for our family and home. The same is true for eating. Consuming too much, too little, or all the wrong kinds of food create health challenges that can also impede our fellowship with God and service to Him.

Food and sleep are gifts from God, given for our enjoyment and the maintenance of our bodies. However, because of our sinful tendencies, these appetites can easily enslave us. In the New Testament, Paul warned the Corinthian believers not to be enslaved by *anything* (1 Cor. 6:12).

So let's examine self-control as it relates to these two bodily appetites—our appetite for food and our appetite for sleep. (I won't address our appetite for sex in this section because I will be covering that topic in the following chapter on purity.)

Eating to the Glory of God

Breakfast is my favorite meal of the day. In fact, I am so fond of breakfast foods that I will occasionally prepare them for dinner! I love to savor a second cup of coffee with a gooey cinnamon roll or homemade toast with jam. At a restaurant, my first choice from the menu is always eggs benedict with a side of fresh berries.

Although I heartily enjoy my breakfast, I usually don't stop to contemplate why I am eating. Maybe you can relate. Most of the time we eat because we are hungry or simply because we desire food (even when we are not hungry). Scripture, however, tells us that we are to eat and drink to the glory of God (1 Cor. 10:31). How then are we to fulfill this command?

First and foremost, we are to receive our food with thanksgiving (1 Tim. 4:3-5). It is God who created and provided food for us in the first place. Shouldn't we at least be grateful? Let us resolve never to eat without offering thanks to our God for His bountiful provision.

God also wants us to enjoy our food. It is a gift from the one "who richly provides us with everything to enjoy" (1 Tim. 6:17). If you study the earthly life of Jesus in the Gospels, you will observe that our Lord enjoyed His food! The Pharisees actually accused Him of being a glutton and a drunkard. Obviously He wasn't, but for the Pharisees to make such an accusation indicates that Jesus thoroughly delighted in the gift of food. So let's relish our food in the same way!

We are to receive food with gratitude and enjoyment; however, we must not be given to overeating. Gluttony (excess in eating) is not a popular term in today's culture, but it is found in Scripture and thus deserves our attention. We find one such example in Proverbs 23:20-21: "Be not among drunkards or among gluttonous eaters of meat, for the drunkard and the glutton will come to poverty, and slumber will clothe them with rags."

Eating too much food is sin. In fact, Proverbs 23:2 recommends drastic measures if we struggle with gluttony: "Put a knife to your throat if you are given to appetite." Obviously the writer of this Proverb isn't literally commanding that we physically harm ourselves. However, the vivid imagery is designed to get our attention and motivate us to exercise self-control.

Eating to calm our fears, alleviate stress, or overcome feelings of depression are other habits that do not glorify God. Food is not our source of help and comfort. God is. In *Love to Eat, Hate to Eat,* Elyse Fitzpatrick notes: "One of the ways that the Spirit's name is translated in Scripture is *Comforter*. He wants to teach you to comfort yourself not with food, but with *His* comfort. His comfort is so winsome, so wholesome, so encouraging—why go anywhere else?"[4]

Finally, we must not allow cultural standards to influence our eating practices. Our society promotes the pursuit of physical beauty, but God's Word exposes this quest as vanity and calls us to pursue the fear of the Lord instead: "Charm is deceitful, and beauty is vain, but a woman who fears the LORD is to be praised" (Prov. 31:30).

Being thin is one of our culture's requirements for physical beauty. However, nowhere in the Bible are we commanded or encouraged to be thin. Therefore, we should examine our eating habits in light of Scripture. We must not chase after the ideal our culture worships, but instead pursue what God esteems.

A disciplined approach to eating does not automatically indicate the presence of self-control as biblically defined. I know a woman who always ordered a salad at restaurants because she desired a figure that would attract the attention of others. Although she appeared disciplined to those around her, this woman realized that her motives were actually sinful. She was pursuing self-glorification—not godliness. This sin of vanity is no less serious than the sin of gluttony. When this woman repented of her vanity, she was then able to pursue self-control in a manner that brought glory to God.

We need to ask ourselves: Am I seeking my own glory or God's glory with my eating habits?

Sleeping to the Glory of God

My husband and I recently discarded our twenty-five-year-old bed frame, box spring, and mattress and bought a new set. On the recommendation of a friend we purchased an adjustable mattress that allowed each of us to choose the level of firmness desired. I have since had many restful, refreshing nights of sleep on our new bed.

Sleep is a gift from God. Scripture says He grants sleep to those He loves (Ps. 127:2), and He makes our sleep sweet (Prov. 3:24). Sleep is a sweet restorer of physical strength. Thus we must make sure to get *enough* sleep daily so that our bodies are fully replenished with the strength they need.

God has designed our bodies to require sleep, and to cut corners may be an expression of pride—an arrogant disregard of our *God-given* physical limitations. God is the only one who does not need sleep. He is the Creator, and we are the created. Therefore, we should humbly embrace our need for sleep—however much we need.

Maybe our temptation related to sleep is not to get too little but to get too much. Proverbs 20:13 has some direct words for those of us in this category: "Love not sleep, lest you come to poverty; open your eyes, and you will have plenty of bread."

If we struggle with overindulgence in the area of sleep, we need to utilize the little "self-control exercise" found in this verse. When the alarm clock rings in the morning, we need to *open our eyes* (and *keep* them open, of course!). However, this will only be possible if we go to bed early enough the night before.

I am often tempted to stay up late at night and indulge in some form of relaxation. But I have been challenged by the frank words of Martha Peace:

> I have heard of women who pride themselves on being "night people." That means they have trouble getting up in the mornings because they come alive at night. They may stay up to all hours reading, watching television, or pursuing some sort of interest. The next morning they are too tired to get up and care for their family. . . .
>
> These women are not "night people." They are lazy and selfish. Who would not rather stay up late to do whatever they pleased and sleep late the next day?
>
> Once a young wife begins getting up earlier than her children and her husband, she will cease to be a "night person." She will be tired at night and go to bed at a reasonable hour so she will be there to serve her family the next morning.[5]

Guilty as charged! How many times I have been one of those "lazy and selfish" women! Rather than using my evening hours to prepare for the next day's work or going to bed early in order to rise early the next morning, I have squandered the time on personal pleasure.

So what time should we go to sleep or wake up each day? That can be determined by knowing how much sleep we need to pursue daily communion with God, care for our husbands and children, and manage the duties of our home. This is applying self-control as it relates to sleep.

Now I must add an addendum for all moms with young children who wake up in the middle of the night. For you, sleep may feel like a lost commodity! However, I can assure you, your children will grow, and eventually you will be able to return to normal sleeping patterns. In the meantime, try to get what sleep you can.

OUR THOUGHTS AND FEELINGS

Take a moment to recall your elation as you walked down the aisle on your wedding day or the happiness you experienced as you held your newborn baby for the first time. Consider the gratitude you felt when your husband received a pay raise or the satisfaction you savored at actually seeing the bottom of the ironing pile! Do you remember your excitement when your friend began to ask questions about the Lord or the wonder *you* experienced the first time Christ revealed His love to you?

Now imagine having those experiences but being unable to think or feel anything. How terrible to conceive of life without the wonderful dynamic of these two gifts! Thoughts and feelings make the experiences of our lives meaningful.

However, as wonderful as our thoughts and feelings may be, they also have been marred by sin. Because of sin, the way we think and feel is often contrary to what Scripture commands. Thus our need for self-control!

It is erroneous to think that if our behavior is exemplary, then it doesn't matter how we think and feel. What we allow to govern our feelings and occupy our thinking will sooner or later determine our behavior. *Sinful thoughts and sinful feelings lead to sinful behavior.* Therefore, we dare not ignore these faculties, but we must exercise self-control in them.

Capturing Our Thoughts

Did you know that an estimated 10,000 thoughts pass through the human mind in a single day? That certainly lends new meaning to the biblical command to "take every thought captive to obey Christ" (2 Cor. 10:5). For not only do we have numerous thoughts, but they also do not easily surrender. We see this reflected in the aggression required: "take every thought *captive.*"

How then do we compel every one of our thoughts to submit to the truth of God's Word? The great twentieth-century preacher D. Martyn Lloyd-Jones gave this wise advice: "Most of your unhappiness in life is due to the fact that you are listening to yourself instead of talking to yourself."[6]

Whenever we are tempted to worry or doubt or fear, we must start talking to ourselves! We should remind ourselves of the truth of God's Word. That is what I needed to do two days ago. I was feverishly working to meet a deadline for this book when my laptop (which is brand-new) began to malfunction. A helpful friend took my computer in for repair, and I hastily transferred my files to the family computer so I could continue to write.

But as I attempted to start again, I discovered I didn't have my glasses. I launched a two-hour search, which concluded with my glasses still missing. All the while my thoughts were running wild. *I don't have time for this. I'll never make that deadline. This book will never get written. God is not going to help me. He doesn't care.*

Were these thoughts consistent with God's Word? Of course not! However, it was a battle to harness my thoughts. The moment I had my unruly thoughts safely captured, I would submit to worry again, and off they'd go like wild bandits! Time and time again I had to stop, pray, confess the sin of anxiety, and seek to replace my sinful thoughts with the truth of God's Word.

I needed to "talk" to myself: *There is always enough time to do what God has called me to do* (Matt. 6:25-27). *God's grace is sufficient* (2 Cor. 12:9). *He is with me, and He will help me* (Isa. 41:10). *He does care* (1 Pet. 5:7).

(Postscript to story: I eventually found my glasses, my laptop was fixed and returned, I met the deadline, and God did help me finish this book!)

In what areas do you struggle with doubt, worry, or fear? What are you tempted to think about that is contrary to truth? Let me encourage you to exercise self-control by rejecting your sinful thoughts and speaking truth to yourself today!

Commanding Our Feelings

Hannah's misery had been building for years, but now it seemed to have reached its peak. Hannah was barren, unable to conceive a child. To make matters worse, her husband had another wife, Peninnah, who bore him many children. And Peninnah constantly sought to "provoke" and "irritate" Hannah because of her disgrace.

Hannah's husband, Elkanah, thought his love alone should be sufficient for her joy. "Am I not more to you than ten sons?" he would ask.

But for Hannah, nothing could compare to having a son. Nothing. *Why doesn't God bless me with a child? I have prayed and waited for so long. Why does God allow me to suffer humiliation and despair?* Hannah gave free rein to her grief and self-pity. She wept bitterly and refused to eat.

Haven't we all found ourselves in a similar state—bitter, angry, and full of despair? Then, of course, we also experience many feelings of surprise, delight, and happiness. If you're anything like me, you can sometimes cover the whole spectrum of emotions in just a few short hours!

As I pointed out earlier, feelings are a gift from God. The Psalms are filled with commands such as, "Delight yourself in the LORD" (Ps. 37:4) and, "Be glad in the LORD" (Ps. 32:11). Paul encouraged the Philippians to "Rejoice in the Lord always." Then, as if once was not enough, he repeated: "Again I will say, Rejoice" (Phil. 4:4). Scripture is clear that the primary purpose of our feelings is to enjoy and glorify God.

But what about those times when, like Hannah, we are *not* experiencing joyful feelings? What if we are feeling anxious, fearful, depressed, resentful, or angry?

We must understand that our feelings are not authoritative. Just because we feel something doesn't make it true. Our feelings are either ruled by truth or ruled by sin. Therefore, we need to discover what is *ruling* our feelings to determine if they are accurate or inaccurate—righteous or sinful.

Although our feelings are not always trustworthy, we are not to ignore them. We shouldn't think: *It doesn't matter how I feel.* It does matter! Our emotions are not morally neutral. Feelings register what is transpiring in our hearts.

We may be inclined to believe that our feelings are caused by life's circumstances or by our body chemistry. Undoubtedly, these things do affect us. However, such factors are not the *source* of sinful feelings. As we encounter life, our emotions are primarily determined by what is in our hearts. *Sinful feelings reveal a sinful heart.* Our story of Hannah (found in 1 Samuel 1) verifies this fact.

When Elkanah found Hannah weeping and in despair, he rebuked her. He asked: "Why is your heart sad?" (v. 8). The literal translation of that question in the Hebrew is: "Why is your heart *bad*?" Essentially, Elkanah was admonishing Hannah for her bitterness.

Hannah responded to Elkanah's correction. She poured out her soul to the Lord (v. 15). Then Hannah "went her way and ate, and her face was no longer sad" (v. 18).

It is important to note in this verse (v. 18) that God still had not answered Hannah's prayer. Nothing about Hannah's circumstances had changed. She still did not have a baby. Yet her crying ceased, her appetite returned, and her countenance radiated peace.

Though we know God did eventually grant Hannah a son, she experienced joy *prior* to that longed-for event. What accounts for Hannah's emotional transformation? How did she go from misery to joy even though she was still barren? Hannah had a heart change. She repented from her bitterness and trusted in God's lovingkindness. This led to joy.

As Christians, our lives are to be characterized by joy. C. S. Lewis once said: "It is a Christian duty, as you know, for everyone to be as happy as he can."[7] We can fulfill this "duty" to be happy by refusing to yield to sinful feelings. Like Hannah, we too can know true joy in the midst of trying circumstances, if we submit our hearts to God's truth.

Self-control is what we need to guard our hearts against sin. And a well-kept heart will beget joyful feelings—the kind of feelings that God intends for us to have.

OUR BEHAVIOR

When we talk about self-control as it relates to our behavior, there are many areas that we could discuss—our speech, our finances, our time, our work—I think you get the idea.

But did you know there is one behavior, if diligently pursued, that will promote self-control in every area of your life? It is not a time-management technique or the latest PDA (which I recently learned from my daughter stands for "personal digital assistant"). It is the daily practice of meeting with God.

Although we all agree that communion with God is a most important practice, we often neglect it in favor of other endeavors. As Charles Spurgeon once said: "It is easier to serve than to commune."[8] And this can be particularly true for us as wives and mothers.

We have the monumental task of feeding, clothing, carpooling, cleaning, doctoring, counseling, encouraging, correcting, training, and coordinating multiple lives at once. Not to mention trying to find time just to take a shower! Sometimes it's easier to wake up and promptly dive into the day. We are tempted to think we don't have time to meet with God. But as John Blanchard points out, we cannot afford to neglect this discipline:

> Surely we only have to be realistic and honest with ourselves to know how regularly we need to turn to the Bible. How often do we face problems, temptation and pressure? EVERY DAY! Then how often do we need instruction, guidance and greater encouragement? EVERY DAY! To catch all these felt needs up into an even greater issue, how often do we need to see God's face, hear his voice, feel his touch, know his power? The answer to all these questions is the same: EVERY DAY![9]

Meeting with God each day is a way of acknowledging that we are totally dependent upon His grace. Psalm 1 eloquently depicts the effect of daily meeting with God: "Blessed is the man . . . [whose] delight is in the law of the LORD, and on his law he meditates day and night. He is like a tree planted by streams of water that yields its fruit in its season, and its leaf does not wither. In all that he does, he prospers."

When we meet with God, we can find peace in the midst of trying circumstances, an eternal perspective where we have lost sight of the truth, and power to fight our battle against sin. We will resemble that tree in Psalm 1 that is healthy, strong, and fruit-bearing. Therefore we should eagerly and consistently respond to our Savior's invitation to come and meet with Him!

NOT ALL BY MYSELF

When my girls were little, I loved to do special projects with them as a way to make memories. One of their favorite projects was to create bunny rabbits out of packaged cinnamon rolls. We would use one round roll for the face and cut another in half for the ears.

The exciting moment came when the girls were allowed to ice their bunnies' ears with pink frosting. Then I helped them add eyes of raisins, a cherry nose, and almond whiskers. When they were finished, they would eagerly show C. J.: "Look, Daddy, I made this *all by myself!*" I would just smile knowingly.

Although it is cute when children assume they can create something "all by themselves," it is altogether different and more serious if we conclude that we can develop self-control "all by ourselves."

In this chapter we have considered self-control as it relates to our eating, our sleeping, our thoughts, our feelings, and our meeting with God. Most likely we are aware of many ways we need to change. Our temptation then is to promptly attempt to manufacture self-control— "all by ourselves." We take a deep breath, muster up fresh resolve, and try again—only harder this time.

But I sincerely hope that is not what you take away from this chapter. That course of action will only lead to failure and despair, once more. However, I want to conclude by pointing your attention back to God and His abundant grace for change. He is eager to help us and has promised to complete the work that He initiated in our lives (Phil. 1:6). But we must choose to be wholly and completely dependent upon Him. As our Lord says: "Apart from me you can do nothing" (John 15:5).

So you see, self-control cannot be achieved "all by ourselves." We develop this virtue only through His "better strength"!

5

The Pleasure of Purity

❧

Several years ago at a church leadership conference, I hosted a panel of pastors' wives at a women's session. We fielded questions on a wide variety of topics—from childrearing to counseling women in crisis situations.

Then a woman from the audience posed the question: "What is one thing you have learned that encourages your husband the most?" As the other women on the panel answered, I pondered my response. *I know what C. J.'s answer would be, but dare I say that?* And then it was my turn. "Make love to him," I blurted out. "That's what my husband would say if he were here!"

The room erupted into a wave of nervous, knowing laughter.

It's true! Engaging in this physical expression of marital intimacy and union is one of the most meaningful ways I can encourage my husband.

If you watch TV, go to the movies, or read magazines today, you can get the idea that the only people having sex (or "good sex") are the ones who aren't married. If marital sex is even portrayed in popular media, it seems bland or routine. Our culture has pushed marital sex into the backroom and instead *celebrates* immoral sex.

That's why younger women today require the training of older, godly women to acquire a biblical perspective on sex. The Greek word for "pure" in our Titus 2 passage means to be holy, innocent, chaste, not contaminated. This word has to do with sexual propriety, avoiding any immorality in thought, word, and action. The word denotes much more than premarital purity. It also includes the concept of sexual purity within marriage.

I've titled this chapter "The Pleasure of Purity" for a specific reason: God intends for us to experience tremendous *joy* and *satisfaction* when we express our sexuality within the confines of marriage. Marital union and fidelity allow a husband and wife to wholly delight in each other, without the consequences and contamination that accompany sinful sex. Purity's pleasure is receiving sex as a wonderful gift from our Creator and enjoying it for His glory.

SEX AND THE SCRIPTURES

Did you realize that an entire book of the Bible is devoted to love, romance, and sexuality in marriage? Think about that! God included the Song of Solomon in the canon of Scripture, His inspired Word.

The eight chapters contained in this little book portray a physical relationship between husband and wife that is filled with uninhibited passion and exhilarating delight. This Song expresses God's heart and intent for our sexual experience. If you have not done so recently, take an hour to read the Song of Solomon and gain a fresh dose of passion for your marriage relationship.

But the Song of Solomon is not the only place in Scripture where God addresses the topic of sex. Let's take a brief tour through the Bible and see what else God has to say!

God's Idea

Mankind didn't invent sex. *God* created and blessed it. It was His idea from the beginning of time. In fact, we only have to read the first two chapters of the Bible before we are introduced to sex:

> So the LORD God caused a deep sleep to fall upon the man, and while he slept took one of his ribs and closed up its place with flesh. And the rib that the LORD God had taken from the man he made into a woman and brought her to the man. Then the man said:

> "This at last is bone of my bones and flesh of my flesh; she shall be called Woman, because she was taken out of Man."

Therefore a man shall leave his father and his mother and hold fast to his wife, and they shall become one flesh. And the man and his wife were both naked and were not ashamed. (Gen. 2:21-25)

God made man and woman to be sexual creatures. God did not wince when Adam, in seeing Eve, was drawn to her sexually. God didn't cringe when Adam and Eve enjoyed sexual relations in the Garden of Eden. In His wise and perfect design, He gave sexual desire to *both* the man and the woman.

Our sexual desire is not evil because God Himself has created it. He is not embarrassed about our sexual nature, and neither should we be embarrassed.

Fashioned for Marriage

God gave sexual desire to both male and female; however, God imposed restrictions upon our sexual appetites. His Word prohibits sexual activity prior to marriage and mandates complete fidelity within marriage (1 Cor. 7:1-9). These boundaries are for our good— so we can enjoy the sheer delight and reap the sweet rewards that flow from obedience to Him.

Intended for Pleasure

The bride in the Song of Solomon eagerly anticipated physical intimacy with her husband: "My beloved put his hand to the latch, and my heart was thrilled within me" (Song 5:4). Hardly the language of a woman indifferent toward sexual relations! This wife exemplifies the pleasure that God intends within the covenant of marriage.

Think about how God created your body. Have you ever stopped to consider why He made the clitoris? It has only one function—to receive and transmit sexual pleasure. God easily could have eliminated this otherwise unnecessary part of our anatomy. But He didn't. He gave us this little organ for no other reason than for sexual enjoyment.

Designed for Intimacy

Prior to the physical union of a man and woman on their wedding night, they do not possess a knowledge characteristic of deep and binding intimacy. They are only acquainted with one another's observable attributes, their most revealed aspects.

The word *know* is often used for marital sex in holy Scripture: "Now Adam *knew* Eve his wife, and she conceived" (Gen. 4:1, emphasis mine). Although a couple may be familiar with one another's likes and dislikes, personal history, character, and beliefs, their knowledge is nonetheless limited. Not until man and woman are joined together in sexual intercourse can they truly "know" the other.

Professor Daniel Akin agrees: "The 'one flesh' relationship (cf. Gen. 2:24) is the most intense, physical intimacy and the deepest, spiritual unity possible between a husband and wife."[1]

Marital sex is the pinnacle of human bonding. It is the highest form of the communication of love—a language that expresses love without words. It calls forth the deepest, most powerful emotions. It creates intimacy within marriage like nothing else. In fact, as we give and receive the gift of lovemaking, this intimacy will grow stronger and more precious as the years go by. Each encounter will lead us to a deeper "knowing" of the one we love.

Created for Procreation

In Genesis 1:27-28 God commanded the man and woman to be fruitful and multiply. Not only is sex a means of intimacy and pleasure in marriage, but God also designed sexual union for the purpose of producing offspring. In doing so, He is working through us in the act of creation!

UNHELPFUL ADVICE

Many Christians through the centuries have not known how to handle our sexuality. Despite the clarity of Scripture, there has been much confusion about how one can be both spiritual and sexual at the same time.

Because of embarrassment, fear, or negative cultural stereotypes, some have tried to ignore sex or forbid its practice within marriage. Others have acknowledged procreation and marriage as honorable but perceived sex for the purpose of pleasure as evil.

One shocking example comes to us from the nineteenth century. In *INSTRUCTION AND ADVICE FOR THE YOUNG BRIDE on the*

Conduct and Procedure of the Intimate and Personal Relationships of the Marriage State for the Greater Spiritual Sanctity of this Blessed Sacrament and the Glory of God, Ruth Smythers, wife of the Reverend L. D. Smythers, wrote the following in 1894:

> To the sensitive young woman who has had the benefits of proper upbringing, the wedding day is ironically, both the happiest and most terrifying day of her life. On the positive side, there is the wedding itself, in which the bride is the central attraction in a beautiful and inspiring ceremony, symbolizing her triumph in securing a male to provide for all her needs for the rest of her life. On the negative side, there is the wedding night, during which the bride must "pay the piper," so to speak, by facing for the first time the terrible experience of sex.
>
> At this point, dear reader, let me concede one shocking truth. Some young women actually anticipate the wedding night ordeal with curiosity and pleasure! Beware such an attitude! A selfish and sensual husband can easily take advantage of such a bride. One cardinal rule of marriage should never be forgotten: GIVE LIT-TLE, GIVE SELDOM, AND ABOVE ALL, GIVE GRUDGINGLY. Otherwise what could have been a proper marriage could become an orgy of sexual lust.

Unbelievable! But Mrs. Smythers didn't stop there.

On the other hand, the bride's terror need not be extreme. While sex is at best revolting and at worst rather painful, it has to be endured, and has been by women since the beginning of time, and is compensated for by the monogamous home and by the children produced through it.

It is useless, in most cases, for the bride to prevail upon the groom to forego the sexual initiation. While the ideal husband would be one who would approach his bride only at her request, and only for the purpose of begetting offspring, such nobility and unselfishness cannot be expected from the average man.

Most men, if not denied, would demand sex almost every day. The wise bride will permit a maximum of two brief sexual experiences weekly during the first months of marriage. As time goes by she should make every effort to reduce this frequency. Feigned illness, sleepiness and headaches are among the wife's best friends in this matter. Arguments, nagging, scolding and bickering also prove very effective if used in the late evening about one hour before the husband would normally commence his seduction.

Clever wives are on the alert for new and better methods of denying and discouraging the amorous overtures of the husband. A good wife should expect to have reduced sexual contacts to once a week by the end of the first year of marriage and to once a month by the end of the fifth year of marriage. By their tenth anniversary many wives have managed to complete their child bearing and have achieved the ultimate goal of terminating all sexual contacts with the husband. By this time, she can depend upon his love for the children and social pressures to hold the husband in the home.[2]

Some very unhelpful advice from our dear Mrs. Smythers! Don't we all feel sorry for *Mr.* Smythers? And for all the husbands of the wives this woman counseled?

Mrs. Smythers's instructions were never God's intent for our sexual relationship. Rather, God's grand design is that man and woman unabashedly enjoy sexual union within marriage!

SEX POLLUTED BY SIN

Undoubtedly, some of you reading this chapter have had past sexual encounters that yielded much pain and confusion. If you have reaped the negative consequences of sexual sin—either as a willing participant or as a victim—be assured that no situation in your life is beyond the reach of God's grace.

Just ask Glenda Revell.

Born out of wedlock to a promiscuous mother who hated her all her life, sexually abused repeatedly by her stepfather, Glenda knew the meaning of suffering. In her book *Glenda's Story: Led By Grace,* she describes her traumatic childhood filled with loneliness, guilt, and despair.

As a young woman, she finally resolved to take her own life, but God graciously rescued her. She "happened" upon a tract explaining the gospel, and on the very day she was going to end her life, she instead put her trust in Christ.

Upon her conversion, Glenda experienced a joy and peace such as she had never known. God provided a church where Scripture was preached and where the family of God cared for her. It was there that she eventually met her husband, David. Today they have a godly marriage and four lovely children.

However, the situation with Glenda's parents never improved. Her mother continued to abuse her verbally until the day she died, and Glenda's stepfather never asked forgiveness for violating her purity.

Despite the anguish of her situation, Glenda's testimony is of the redeeming power of Christ. "Sexual defilement of a child is a monstrous sin," she writes,

> and the rape of a child's spirit is on equal footing. The damage from either would appear irreversible. But as Dr. David Jeremiah has said, "Our God has the power to reverse the irreversible." It is true, for I have tasted of His cure from both, and it fills me with a longing for Him that the happiest of childhoods could not have given.[3]

The "cure" that Glenda refers to is the cross of Christ.

> He showed me Calvary once more. . . . I saw the horror of my sin, nailing the Son of God to that miserable cross, torturing Him, mocking Him, spitting on Him. Yet He had forgiven me freely. No one had committed such atrocities against me. How could I do anything less than forgive?
>
> Forgiveness came. And with it came healing, complete peace and freedom—absolute freedom—to serve my God and to enjoy His love and peace now and forevermore.[4]

Maybe you can relate to Glenda's horrendous childhood, or possibly you carry around guilt from your own past sexual sin. Perhaps it is your husband's past or present sin that looms large in your heart and mind. You may wonder if you will ever be free from the guilt, fear, and despair.

But no matter how distorted your view or traumatic your experience, help is available. I would encourage you as a couple to pursue biblical counseling from your pastor and his wife. Because of the transforming power of Jesus Christ, even the most difficult and painful situation can be turned into a story of grace.

THE PROBLEM OF LUST

Not only do we experience the consequences of past sexual sin, but we also encounter the ever-present temptation to lust. Sexual temptation is no respecter of persons. You can be male or female, young or old, rich or poor, single or married, happily married or unhappily married. *No one* is safe from this vice.

In fact, we should not be surprised or shocked if we ourselves are tempted sexually. The Bible has already warned us that temptation is inevitable. First Corinthians 10:13 says, "No temptation has overtaken you that is not common to man."

Several years back when C. J. and I were visiting England, the media spotlight was on an evangelical leader whose sexual immorality had recently been discovered. In response to this moral failure, a newspaper columnist wrote the following:

> A few years ago, I was in a remote part of the world, alone with the owner of an idyllic island. As the days went by, he became more attentive and more attractive. It was an extremely pleasant sensation. I was enjoying myself greatly. My work required me to be there and my head insisted that I was above temptation. But I'm not. The Bible tells me so.
>
> Consequently I knew I must leave urgently. I did. By the grace of God, I didn't commit adultery. Not then and not yet. But, it's there in my heart biding its time. Jesus said that makes me as bad as the worst offender. Happily, because I have always been taught that I am capable of adultery, I've always been on my guard against it. After all, it doesn't start when you jump into bed with your lover. But months, years earlier, when you tell yourself that your friend understands you better than your spouse.[5]

What keen insight! Let us never assume we are above temptation. We must pay close attention to the warning of 1 Corinthians 10:12: "Therefore let anyone who thinks that he stands take heed lest he fall."

A CLARION CALL FOR PURITY

Because of our propensity to commit sexual sin and spoil God's wonderful gift of sex, we must resolve to walk in absolute purity. This commitment requires no small effort on our part. Elisabeth Elliot alerts us to the nature of this battle:

If there is an Enemy of Souls (and I have not the slightest doubt that there is), one thing he cannot abide is the desire for purity. Hence a man or woman's passions become his battleground. The Lover of Souls does not prevent this. I was perplexed because it seemed to me He should prevent it, but He doesn't. He wants us to learn to use our weapons.[6]

God does not "prevent" our conflict with sin. Rather He directs us to draw upon His inexhaustible supply of grace so that we can resist sexual temptation and grow in purity. The following are three tactics we must employ in this battle for our soul.

Set Our Hearts and Minds on Things Above

As we learned from Glenda's testimony, it was only through the cross that she obtained freedom from her sin. The same is true for us in our quest for purity. Take note of the significant progression in Colossians 3:1-5:

> If then you have been raised with Christ, seek the things that are above, where Christ is, seated at the right hand of God. Set your minds on things that are above, not on things that are on earth. For you have died, and your life is hidden with Christ in God. When Christ who is your life appears, then you also will appear with him in glory. Put to death therefore what is earthly in you: sexual immorality, impurity, passion, evil desire, and covetousness, which is idolatry.

Did you catch which comes first? Before we attempt to put to death sexual immorality, impurity, evil desire, etc., in our lives, we must first seek things that are above. Growth in purity can only be realized as we look upward to Jesus Christ.

Does that mean we minimize or dismiss impurity in our lives? Does this indicate that God is tolerant of evil desire or sexual immorality? Of course not! God neither makes light of nor ignores our sin. He hates sin. That is why Jesus had to die on the cross. Our Savior's death not only secures our forgiveness for sin, but also demands our departure from sin and provides us with the power we need to overcome sin (2 Cor. 5:14-15; Rom. 6:6-7).

Let us never forget to put first things first. Our conquest of sin begins with a deliberate resolve to set our hearts and minds on things above. As we contemplate what Christ has done for us, we will be compelled to pursue purity for His glory.

Make No Provision for the Flesh

It is the close of another long day. In fact, you feel like yesterday never really ended. The baby was up five times during the night. The toddler was cranky all afternoon. You accidentally burned dinner, and the evening culminated with a conflict between you and your husband.

But now your family is finally asleep, and you want to escape from all the unpleasantness of your day. So you flip on the TV "just to see what's on." A show piques your interest, and you pause with your finger on the remote. Although you know this program can be vulgar at times, it's the only amusing thing on, and you think you deserve a little leisure time. You promptly dismiss your conscience and settle down to enjoy yourself.

This scenario I've just described may or may not be a familiar temptation to you. Regardless, Scripture teaches that we *all* have areas where we are susceptible. In Romans 13:14 we read: "Put on the Lord Jesus Christ, and make no provision for the flesh, to gratify its desires." In response to this verse, each of us needs to ask: When, where, and with whom are we most tempted to accommodate our flesh and gratify its desires?

Now I am not insinuating that rest or leisure activities are sinful. God's Word actually *requires* us to rest, and there are many God-honoring activities that provide us with refreshment!

However, I *am* insisting from God's Word that we never indulge our sinful desires in our recreational pursuits. For example, we should not read anything, view anything, or listen to anything that arouses impure thoughts or compromises our biblical convictions. *That* would be sinful!

Observe David's commitment in Psalm 101:2-3 (NIV): "I will walk in my house with blameless heart. I will set before my eyes no vile thing." The psalmist's resolve was sweeping—*no vile thing*. Notice also that David determined to walk with a blameless heart *at home*. As Charles Spurgeon once said: "What we are at home, that we are indeed."[7]

So can we say like David, "I will walk in my house with blameless heart"? Have we purposed not to see, read, or hear any vile thing? Or are we taking liberties where we shouldn't? Do we watch any unwholesome movies or television programs? Do we read worthless materials—such as romance novels or magazines—that tempt us to sinful fantasies? Do we listen to ungodly music that stirs up impure thoughts? If we answered yes to any one of these three questions, we must expunge these practices from our lifestyle.

Paul told Timothy to flee youthful passions (2 Tim. 2:22). In 1 Corinthians 6:18, we are exhorted to flee sexual immorality. This verb *flee* denotes a very strong reaction to temptation. It is not enough to simply *walk* away. We are to *run* away from temptation as fast as we can, to take flight. And we're deceived if we think we're strong enough to handle it. We wouldn't be urged to flee temptation if it were something we could manage.

A woman once told me that she stopped going to her male hairdresser because she found him to be attractive. That became a distraction when she would go for a haircut. Despite the fact that he gave her the best haircut she had ever received, and even though there had never been any inappropriate interaction between them, she determined that she would not fool with temptation. Instead, she found a new hairdresser. That's an example of what it means to flee temptation!

It is crucial that we identify the times, places, people, and sources that can present us with sexual temptation. And we must devise a biblical strategy in order to make *no* provision for our flesh.

Be Honest and Pursue Accountability

Remember the response of Adam and Eve after they sinned against God in the Garden of Eden? They hid from Him. They evaded personal responsibility for their disobedience.

Guess what? You and I struggle with the same tendency; we are inclined to hide. Like Adam and Eve, we seek to avoid owning up to our sin.

Yet to attempt to hide our sin and escape blame are perilous endeavors. We will not grow in purity if we pursue such practices, and that is one reason why God has established the local church. It is through relationships with other Christians in our church that we can receive counsel, support, and encouragement in our struggle against sin.

If we are facing sexual temptation, it is imperative that we pursue mature and godly friendships in our local church. We should ask people to pray for us, challenge us, and hold us accountable to God's Word.

So let's not hide our sin, but rather honestly confess it and ask others for help. As we humble ourselves in this way, God will use our friends' encouragement and correction to help us grow in purity.

THREE PRINCIPLES FOR "GRADE A" PASSION

Our quest for purity inextricably involves the ardent pursuit of an exciting sexual relationship with our husbands. Marital relations are an essential part of God's plan to protect us from temptation to sinful lust (1 Cor. 7:2-5).

The Bible does not give explicit instructions regarding marital sex. However, it does provide us with *principles* to guide our behavior. So let us consider three biblical principles for cultivating a passionate marriage.

Be Attractive

"In mine eye she is the sweetest lady that ever I looked on,"[8] said young Claudio of his beloved Hero, in Shakespeare's comedy *Much Ado About Nothing*.

The husband in Song of Solomon was also captivated by his wife's beauty. "How beautiful and pleasant you are," he enthused, "O loved one, with all your delights!" (Song 7:6). As wives, we should aim to be beautiful in *our* husbands' eyes, and theirs alone.

Often women who meticulously attended to their physical appearance before marriage neglect it once the wedding ceremony is over. I once overheard a woman negatively comment about another woman's appearance: "She looks married." Ouch! That shouldn't be! We should give the same careful attention to our physical appearance *after* marriage as we did *before*.

We need to discover what makes us attractive to our husbands. What clothing, hairstyle, or makeup do they find most appealing? And we should strive to care for our appearance—not only when we go out, but also at home where only our husbands see us.

Now I must also acknowledge the reality that physical beauty is passing away. After ten, twenty, or fifty years of marriage, we will not look as lovely as we did on our wedding day!

However, we are given some wonderful news in 1 Peter 3:3-5. It declares that if we cultivate a gentle and quiet spirit, we will actually make ourselves beautiful. Although it doesn't explain how this happens, and it certainly is not referring to physical beauty, it does assert that we will become more attractive as we grow in godly character.

Elisabeth Elliot is a woman who displays this extraordinary beauty. I had the privilege of meeting this author and speaker several years ago. Although she was in her seventies at the time, her regal appearance fascinated me. She had the gray hair and wrinkles that accompany old age, and yet she was remarkably beautiful.

This is because Elisabeth Elliot has cultivated the *unfading* beauty of a gentle and quiet spirit. And this same godly beauty will make *us* attractive to our husbands, even as our physical beauty fades through the years.

Be Available

Contrary to Mrs. Smytherss's advice to "give little, give seldom, and above all, give grudgingly," Scripture makes it plain that my body belongs to my husband, and his body belongs to me.

The husband and wife in the Song of Solomon understood this principle: "I am my beloved's and my beloved is mine" (Song 6:3). And in 1 Corinthians 7:3-5 we read:

> *The husband should give to his wife her conjugal rights, and likewise the wife to her husband. For the wife does not have authority over her own body, but the husband does. Likewise the husband does not have authority over his own body, but the wife does. Do not deprive one another, except perhaps by agreement for a limited time, that you may devote yourselves to prayer; but then come together again, so that Satan may not tempt you because of your lack of self-control.*

As husband and wife, we belong entirely and unreservedly to each other—my body is his possession, and his body is mine. We are to give ourselves without qualification and not withhold the pleasure of sex.

The only exception to this rule is for the activity of prayer and then only by mutual agreement and for a limited time.

As wives, we must heed this admonition and offer no excuses. One man has observed, "I've heard many excuses for not having sex— not in the mood, headache, too tired, don't have time. Prayer and fasting has never been one of them."[9]

When we choose to obey God and give our bodies to our husbands—even if we don't feel like it—God will reward us with pleasure. As Elisabeth Elliot encourages us: "The essence of sexual enjoyment for a woman is self-giving. . . . You will find that it is impossible to draw the line between giving pleasure and receiving pleasure. If you put the giving first, the receiving is inevitable."[10]

Be Anticipatory

It has been said that the sexiest organ of the human body lies between our ears. Our brains have a tremendous effect on our sexual experience. How we think influences our sexual desire.

Most of us will confess that before marriage our sexual desire was strong. It was hard *not* to anticipate the wedding night and that first opportunity to express our passion.

But what about now? When was the last time we spent all day looking forward to physical relations with our husbands? If it has been awhile, if we no longer anticipate lovemaking as we once did, it may be that we have stopped fantasizing about our husbands. When we neglect to think sexual thoughts, we should not be surprised by our lack of sexual desire.

On the other hand, fantasizing about our husbands throughout the day will heighten our sexual longing. In case you are wondering, it is perfectly holy to think these erotic, sensual thoughts. Let's take our cue from the wife in Song of Solomon:

My beloved is radiant and ruddy, distinguished among ten thousand. His head is the finest gold; his locks are wavy, black as a raven. His eyes are like doves besides streams of water, bathed in milk, sitting beside a full pool. His cheeks are like beds of spices, mounds of sweet-smelling herbs. His lips are lilies, dripping liquid myrrh. His arms are rods of gold, set with jewels. His body is polished ivory, bedecked with sapphires. His legs are alabaster columns, set on bases of gold. His

*appearance is like Lebanon, choice as the cedars. His mouth is most
sweet, and he is altogether desirable. (Song 5:10-16)*

This wife's sensual musings culminated in the exclamation:
"He is altogether desirable." Do you see how her passion was
ignited by fantasizing about her husband? God has furnished us
with imaginations, and we should use them to "daydream" about
our husbands.

Another common reason for a lack of sexual desire is fatigue.
Although weariness is a potential reality in many seasons of our lives,
it is probably most pronounced when a woman is caring for small
children.

Recently I had a conversation with a young first-time mother.
"Before our baby was born," she explained, "I had plenty of time to
romance my husband, clean my home, and cook delicious meals. But
now there are days I'm still in my bathrobe at three o'clock in the afternoon, because I've spent all morning caring for our newborn! So how
do I keep my husband a priority when my child requires so much time
and attention?" she asked.

"Honey," I replied, "fix your husband a peanut butter and jelly
sandwich for dinner and give him great sex after dinner, and he will
feel prized by you!"

My response was an attempt to encourage her to curtail her
efforts in other areas so she could devote herself to what pleased her
husband the most. For many husbands, "great sex" would top their
list! They would happily do without the gourmet meals and immacu-
late home if it meant we saved our energy for sex. So let me encourage you to ask your husband what is most meaningful to him!

If we struggle with fatigue, let's evaluate our lifestyles. Do we need
to scale back on tasks of lesser importance? Do we need to pare down
our schedules? Do we need to take a nap during the day? Do we need
to take a shower before lovemaking? Do we need to vary the time of
day we make love? Granted, this requires some pretty creative planning, but it's vital that we make these changes if we are to anticipate
lovemaking.

By now I hope you realize where all this "anticipation" is headed.
Our longing should culminate in what Proverbs 5:19 describes as
intoxicating sex! Husbands desire more than merely having their bio-

logical needs met by a bored, passive wife. Rather, they delight in our initiation of the lovemaking experience, and they derive great pleasure when we are eager and excited during the act. But don't just take my word for it! Ask your husband today what would most enhance the sexual experience for him.

Let me add here that I have occasionally counseled women whose husbands had less desire for sexual relations than they had. This challenging situation can often produce confusion, pain, and even fear. However, it need not hinder you from pursuing a God-glorifying marriage. Again, I would encourage you and your husband to seek godly counsel from your pastor and his wife. And remember to put your trust in God: He is at work in your marriage for your good and His glory (Rom. 8:28).

THE PLEASURE OF PURITY

"One of the greatest gifts a person can give his or her mate in marriage is exclusive and exciting sex,"[11] writes Dr. Daniel Akin. As we have discovered in this chapter, "exclusive sex"—purity within the marriage covenant—is intended by God, not to inhibit our pleasure, but to enhance our pleasure. Making ourselves attractive, being available, and anticipating lovemaking will all foster "exciting sex" with our spouse!

However, having taught this material on numerous occasions, I am aware that not all wives will be thrilled with this message. Perhaps you are one of them. "Pleasure" might not be uppermost in your mind as you contemplate this topic. Maybe this was the chapter your husband most wanted you to read—and the one you most wanted to avoid.

Are you weighed down by a lack of faith? *My sexual desire will never approximate that of my husband's!* Do you feel immobilized by the amount of deficiency that has been exposed? *I will never be able to make all those changes!* Or does past or present sexual sin still appear as an insurmountable obstacle in your view? *My situation is beyond all hope!*

May I implore you not to despair? These thoughts and feelings are contrary to the truth of God's Word. Please be persuaded that God is able to renew your sexual desire, empower you to change, and revive you with hope. You can trust the Savior to gradually transform your sexual relationship with your husband. Remember that sex was God's idea in the first place, and He is passionately committed to blessing the marriage bed, for our pleasure and His glory.

In conclusion, I cannot think of more fitting, moving words to leave you with than those of Robert Farrar Capon:

> The bed is the heart of the home, the arena of love, the seedbed of life, and the one constant point of meeting. It is the place where, night-by-night, forgiveness and fair speech return that the sun may not go down on our wrath; where the perfunctory kiss and the entirely ceremonial pat on the backside become unction and grace. It is the oldest, friendliest thing in anybody's marriage, the first used and the last left, and no one can praise it enough.[12]

6

The Honor of Working at Home

❧

I was sitting in the doctor's office, staring at the blank space on the patient form labeled "Occupation," trying to decide what to write. I wasn't having difficulty remembering what I do. My "occupation" has been the same for the past twenty-eight years. And it wasn't a tricky word to spell. A third grader could jot it down.

So why was I having so much trouble filling in a tiny space on a piece of paper that required a simple one-word answer? The reason, you see, is that I am a homemaker by profession, and I was embarrassed to admit that is what I do.

Now I certainly had no intention of lying on the form, but I was trying to think of a creative way to make homemaker sound more important. Then the thought struck me: *I am more concerned about the opinion of the individual who will read this questionnaire than I am about the approval of the One who has called me to be a homemaker.* I had succumbed to worldly thinking rather than viewing my profession as the Bible portrays it—a high calling from God.

I quietly repented before God as I sat in the doctor's waiting room that day and promptly and proudly wrote down "homemaker" in the little empty box.

EVERYTHING HAS CHANGED

Maybe you are a homemaker. If so, chances are you can relate to my hesitation. You too have wanted to skip over the "occupation" space on forms. Or perhaps it's your husband's office Christmas party you dread—where countless times in a single evening you face the obligatory question: "So where do *you* work?"

Or maybe you endure a constant barrage of advice from well-meaning relatives: "You are still young and have so much potential. You shouldn't be wasting all your talent by staying at home. You need to go out and make something of your life."

Author Danielle Crittenden notes that "whether it's the pleasure of being a wife or of raising children or of making a home—[these] were, until the day before yesterday, considered the most natural things in the world."[1]

But all that has changed. Women today are perplexed and uncertain as to how to approach these aspects of life. And much of this confusion is a direct result of the feminist ideology that has permeated our society. In her book *What Our Mothers Didn't Tell Us,* Mrs. Crittenden describes what the feminist movement concretely built into a generation of women:

> For more than thirty years the women's movement has told us that we would be happier, more fulfilled human beings if we left our homes and children and went out to work. To the degree that we might feel misgivings or guilt about leaving our babies to others to raise, we have been assured that such feelings are imposed upon us by society, and sexist—no more normal for a mother to experience than a father. Instead, we've been taught to suppress these worries and to put our work ahead of our families, or at the very least, to attempt to "balance" the demands of boss and baby.[2]

And with this message, feminists have been, in Crittenden's words, "spectacularly persuasive." The percentage of American women with children under eighteen who have entered the workforce has steadily increased. By 2001, 73.1 percent of these women were in the labor force, up from 66.7 percent in 1990 and 56.6 in 1980.[3]

THE HOMEMAKER'S POPULARITY CRISIS

Part and parcel of the feminist message has been "a disdain of domesticity and a contempt for housewives."[4] The volume level of this hostility was particularly shrill and piercing in the early years of the women's movement. However, its echo still rings in our ears today.

Consequently, the profession of homemaking is not very popular these days. It has dropped very low on our society's chart of worthwhile contributions—if it even makes the list at all! Many women are reluctant to stay at home because of the lack of respect they receive from our culture. Homemaking is deemed a low-status job.

Bonnie Barker, a homemaker in my church, recently encountered this bias in the form of an article in our local newspaper. This article featured a ten-year old girl, also from our church, who had received an award at the county fair. Bonnie was eager to read the piece but found herself disappointed by the journalist's perspective. She sent the following letter in response:

> Dear Ms. _____:
> Last week I was so delighted to sit down and read the article you wrote about Brielle Nelson, the Montgomery County Fair's "Baker of the Year." But as I read through your article, I was saddened and disappointed when you referred to the many people who entered the Home Arts as "homebodies and underachievers." For a moment I felt a metaphorical "stab in the heart" since being a "stay at home" mother of five, I seemed to qualify for this arbitrary (yet false) category you set up. But, I wanted to give you the benefit of the doubt, so I read on. You set out to prove that not all are such underachievers as those who stay at home but went on to feature women who hold important positions in our society. I certainly don't argue that such women have achieved much, but I think you have missed a key opportunity to feature what has really helped to make Brielle Nelson so successful. You see, I have had the joy of knowing the Nelson family personally for a number of years. Brielle's mother, Margaret, has set aside the accolades of corporate life, the career path, the paychecks, the bonuses, the applause of our current society to stay at home and seriously invest her life in the next generation. To top it all off, the children she is "underachieving" for are all adopted. Figure that!! Where do you think Brielle learned to bake so well? It certainly wasn't in the orphanage. I know it had

a lot to do with a "homebody" (uh, may I say homemaker?) who has poured out her life selflessly into her children so that they will hopefully have a seriously positive impact on our society for generations to come.

If I may, I would like to humbly submit alternative words to describe all of us "homebodies and underachievers." How about homemakers and visionaries?

For Your Consideration,
Bonnie Barker, Homemaker

The journalist's depiction of homemakers as "homebodies and underachievers" is just one example of our culture's perspective—not exactly favorable or encouraging! In fact, you get the feeling nowadays that doing anything outside of the home is more honorable than working in the home. Dorothy Patterson characterizes the current mindset in this way:

> Much of the world would agree that being a housekeeper is acceptable as long as you are not caring for your own home; treating men with attentive devotion would also be right as long as the man is the boss in the office and not your husband; caring for children would even be deemed heroic service for which presidential awards could be given as long as the children are someone else's and not your own.[5]

THE FAILURE OF FEMINISM

Though the feminist movement has succeeded in undermining the role of the homemaker and driving her into the workforce, it has not secured her happiness and fulfillment. Again quoting Danielle Crittenden:

> Women today enjoy unprecedented freedom and opportunity. So why, I'd wondered, were the articles in women's magazines so relentlessly pessimistic? I'd pulled thirty years' worth of back issues of *Mademoiselle, Glamour, Vogue, Redbook, Cosmopolitan,* and *McCall's* from the stacks of the Library of Congress. It was partly from reading magazines like these that Betty Friedan had concluded in 1963 that the women of her generation felt unhappy and stifled. A huge social transformation had taken place between Friedan's day and mine. Had it made women any happier? If the truth about women can be found in the magazines they buy, then the answer was, resoundingly, no. In fact, these magazines por-

trayed my contemporaries as even more miserable and insecure, more thwarted and obsessed with men, than the most depressed, Lithium-popping, suburban reader of the 1950s.[6]

Feminism has failed to deliver as advertised. Yet feminist philosophy has become thoroughly integrated into the values of mainstream society—so much so, that it has been absorbed and applied by the majority of women, even many who do not consider themselves feminist.

This is not altogether surprising. We should expect women who are unaware of the truth of the gospel to be confused and misguided about their identity and calling. But what is surprising and distressing is how many Christian women have been seduced by the feminist doctrine. Not a few Christian wives and mothers have joined the women of our culture in the mass exodus from their homes.

Because we have breathed toxic feminist air for several decades now, we cannot ignore the fact that its poison has potentially infected us all—particularly in relation to homemaking, or, as our Titus 2 passage calls it, "working at home." We must return to Scripture to discover what God requires of us in this command.

Let's pray that God would enable each of us to approach His Word with a humble heart, quickly admitting any attitudes or actions we discover contrary to His mandate to work at home and resolutely changing.

THE BIBLE AND THE HOME

So what *does* God's Word have to say to wives and mothers about working at home? First, the obvious conclusion we can draw from the Titus 2 command—to be "working at home"—is that *the principal place of work for wives and mothers is at home.* Also, in 1 Timothy Paul counseled the younger widows to marry, bear children, and *manage their households* (1 Tim. 5:14). Then we have the noble woman in Proverbs 31, whom Scripture puts forth as the ideal wife and mother: *Home* was her sphere of work.

Scripture is clear that men are responsible to be the providers for the home (1 Tim. 5:8), while women are responsible to be the caretakers of the home. Now the Bible does not say that wives and mothers are never allowed to work outside the four walls of their houses; nor does it preclude them from receiving wages for work. Scripture provides examples of godly women who worked in other settings and earned extra income, but never to the neglect of their families and homes.

The Proverbs 31 woman is one such model. During her lifetime she pursued many endeavors beyond the confines of her house. She worked among the poor and needy, she traveled, she bought real estate and planted vineyards, she made linen garments and sashes and sold them, she participated in trading—but her primary motive and goal with all these enterprises was to serve her family and home. This woman's attentiveness to her home is God's standard for our conduct. *Working at home must always remain a constant and ongoing priority in our lives.*

May I interject here an exhortation to single women reading this chapter? I can understand how easy it would be to make school or the workplace the priority in your life. Yet the call to make the home a priority extends to all women, no matter your season in life. Even now you can discover ways to make your residence a home, cultivate the domestic arts, and prayerfully consider how to use your home for outreach and care to others.

A HEART FOR THE HOME

Since God orders our lives in seasons, there will be periods of time when pursuits outside the home will not compromise the quality of our work in the home. Obviously, a woman whose children are grown and gone or a woman who does not have children has more discretionary time for efforts beyond her home than a woman with three small children.

But whenever we contemplate opportunities outside of the home, we must first consider what consequences they might have on our families. We must also evaluate our motives. We should ask ourselves questions such as:

"What are my reasons for considering this opportunity? Are they selfish or God-honoring?"

"Will pursuing this venture glorify God and honor the gospel?"

"Is this an undertaking that will help my husband?"

"Will it enhance and enrich the lives of my family?"

"Does this endeavor hinder my role as caretaker of my home?"

Questions like these will help us to make wise decisions, for it is imperative that we never lose sight of our primary obligation to our homes.

Now I must pause here and acknowledge that there are wives and mothers in unusual and challenging circumstances who have no choice but to work outside the home. Two such women are friends of mine. They work full-time jobs, not in order to pursue selfish ambitions, but out of necessity. In fact, they would prefer to be full-time homemakers.

Cindy's husband suffers from a debilitating disease that forced him to stop working over ten years ago. Since then Cindy has had to assume the role of breadwinner for her family and lay aside her desire to stay at home. But even though she works a forty-hour week at her job, Cindy's passion and delight for her home has not diminished:

> I see my first priority as being a wife and homemaker. Even though I have to work, that is a secondary calling. I want to make my home a place of rest, peace, and order. I want it to be a haven where God's character is reflected through my actions and speech as well as my creative giftings.

My other friend Kim is a single mom who reentered the workforce when her husband left her with two small daughters to raise. A new Christian at the time, Kim struggled to maintain a heart for her home and work at the same time. "I lost sight of the home in my selfishness. I felt I deserved rest and relaxation or a dinner out even when there wasn't the money," she says.

A woman in my church took Kim under her wing and inspired her to develop a love for her home. Kim recalls that "Leslie's example of passion and love for her family helped me to redirect my gaze. I came to see caring for my home as God's role for me. I also realized that I needed to invest in my home in order to set a godly example for my girls. And as I made those changes, I grew to love my home."

Kim's investment paid off. Today both her girls are grown and married and caring for homes of their own!

I have known both Cindy and Kim for many years, and I admire their devotion to the task of homemaking. They have created lovely homes for their families and have served many people through gracious hospitality.

Maybe you identify with my friends' stories. Your earnest desire is to be a full-time homemaker; yet you bear the burden of providing financially for your family. Most likely this dual responsibility leaves you exhausted and depleted.

But may I direct your attention to the sustaining grace of God? Psalm 28:7 reminds us: "The LORD is my strength and my shield; in him my heart trusts, and I am helped." God is the One who has called you to be a homemaker, and He will supply all the strength you need as you look to Him.

RULER OF THE HOUSE

Martin Luther, the man who sparked the Protestant Reformation, once quipped about his wife: "In domestic affairs I defer to Katie. Otherwise I am led by the Holy Ghost."[7] While facetious, Luther's comment holds biblical credibility. As wives, we *are* to be in charge of domestic affairs!

The command in Titus 2 to be "working at home" is further illuminated by 1 Timothy 5:14 where Paul says: "So I would have younger widows marry, bear children, *manage their households*, and give the adversary no occasion for slander" (emphasis mine).

In the Greek, the phrase "manage their households" carries a strong connotation. It literally means to be the ruler, despot, or master of the house. So we see that "working at home" means we are to function as the home manager—taking full ownership for all the domestic duties of the household.

Once again the woman in Proverbs 31 is our example. She presided over the entire range of responsibilities in her home. She helped her husband; cared for her children; completed chores; supervised servants; oversaw land; invested money; bought, sold, and traded goods (just to name a few duties!). The Proverbs 31 wife maintained a broad sphere of rule in her household.

Imitating this woman's model, Sarah Edwards, the wife of the eighteenth-century preacher Jonathan Edwards, managed her household with careful and thorough diligence. One day Dr. Edwards emerged from his studies and asked his wife: "Isn't it about time for the hay to be cut?" To which Sarah was able to respond, "It's been in the barn for two weeks."[8]

Sarah created a world where her husband could fulfill his God-given duties without being concerned for the domestic tasks of the home. We should aspire to do likewise!

Now with the command to "rule" in our homes, I must provide two cautions. First of all, this is not license to usurp our husband's authority. Our management in the home must be carried out in complete support of his leadership and direction.

But this mandate also precludes the currently popular "co-responsibility" approach to homemaking. As wives, it is *our* job to manage our homes, and we should not expect our husbands to contribute equally to this task.

This is not to say that our husbands shouldn't help around the house. There are times when we legitimately need their assistance, and this is especially true for moms with small children. The point is not to excuse our husbands from service in the home, but rather to solidify our role as manager of the home. God has given that assignment to us!

And in case the magnitude of this assignment makes you feel as if a load of bricks has just been deposited on your back, cheer up! This calling from God is not intended to be a burden, but rather a source of great fulfillment and joy. Even if we do not think of ourselves as administrators, as organized or capable of managing anything, and although we might not be as gifted as Sarah Edwards or the woman in Proverbs 31, God has equipped each of us with the skills we need to efficiently manage *our* homes.

For in truth, we are unable to rule effectively in our own strength. It is God who supplies all the time, energy, and ability we need to glorify Him as home managers.

CONTINUING EDUCATION

Individuals dedicated to their careers commonly pursue additional learning opportunities to brush up on a skill or acquire a new skill. We should approach our occupation as home managers with the same seriousness and commitment to excellence.

We should never suppose that we have achieved ideal homemaker status or remain content with merely adequate job performance. But we should always strive to update, improve, and sharpen our home-making skills.

I don't know about you, but when I embarked upon the career of homemaking, I had a lot to learn (and I still do!). So in order to grow more competent as a homemaker, I have pursued multiple avenues of instruction.

Over the years I have purchased or borrowed countless books on topics such as cleaning, organizing, or decorating. Along with my daughters, I have enrolled in cooking classes through the county or lessons at the local craft store. I have sought practical knowledge from other women in my church who excel in various aspects of the domestic arts. And after I am finished writing this book, there is more I want to learn. I hope to master our family's budgeting software and discover how to save time and money by more effectively utilizing the Internet.

So I hope you see that homemaking is not a dead-end occupation that requires little ability or provides minimal challenge. As Dorothy Patterson asserts:

> Homemaking—being a full-time wife and mother—is not a destructive drought of uselessness but an overflowing oasis of opportunity; it is not a dreary cell to contain one's talents and skills but a brilliant catalyst to channel creativity and energies into meaningful work.[9]

HOW MAY I HELP YOU?

With any managerial role—whether in a large company or the local McDonald's—a job description is essential. Scripture has provided a job description for us as managers of our homes, and it is surprisingly simple! We are to be our husband's helper (Gen. 1:26-31; 2:7-25; 1 Cor. 11:8-9). As Douglas Wilson elaborates:

> The man needs *the* help; the woman needs *to* help. Marriage was created by God to provide companionship in the labor of domin-ion. The cultural mandate, the requirement to fill and subdue the earth, is still in force, and a husband cannot fulfill this portion of the task in isolation. He needs a companion suitable for him in the work to which God has called him. He is called to the work and must receive help from her. She is called to the work through min-

istering to him. *He is oriented to the task, and she is oriented to him.*[10] (emphasis mine)

When we understand that our main objective as home managers is to be oriented to our husbands, this clarifies our responsibilities. We can easily determine what we should do and how we should do it by asking ourselves: "What will most help my husband?" The answer to this question is usually obvious and uncomplicated.

My problem is, I often don't ask the question!

In fact, I have come to see that I frequently make choices, pursue endeavors, and carry out duties in my home in a manner that serves *me*, instead of in a way that helps my husband.

Let me tell you about one such episode. It seemed like a good idea at the time. My friend Andrea had just given birth to her first child, and I was eager to serve her. So I promptly volunteered to make her a meal. Sounds harmless enough, right? Perhaps even downright noble? Well, it wasn't.

You see, not only did I fail to consult with my husband before offering my services, but I did not even pause to consider the effect this might have on my family. It was an unusually busy season for my husband and me, and I was already juggling more than I could handle. So adding the time it would take to prepare this meal meant I was destined to drop something. The first priority to go would most likely be my care for my husband and children.

When I finally informed C. J. of my philanthropic intentions, he kindly pointed out that this was not the most convenient time for my initiative. I knew he was right.

The more I thought about it, the more I came to see what was truly motivating me. Far from being honorable or praiseworthy, my reasons for making this meal were actually selfish. I was trying to impress Andrea and draw attention to myself. I wanted her to think that I was a great friend, at least as good a friend as the next woman!

After recognizing my self-promoting agenda, I chose a different course of action. I still provided Andrea's family with a meal, but instead of wowing her with my culinary skills, I purchased dinner from a local restaurant. But just think—I could have avoided this entire ordeal if only I had asked the question: "What will most help my husband?"

HELPING OURSELVES

Orienting our lives to our husbands not only helps them, but it helps us as well! When we adapt our lifestyles to serve our husbands, it helps to keep our schedules manageable. Oftentimes we feel pulled in multiple directions by the demands of family, friends, church, school, and community—not to mention our own desires! We try to please everyone, only to feel frustrated and frazzled at the end of the day. However, when we build our lives around helping our husbands, all other "needs" have to assume their proper place on our calendars—that is, if they even belong there at all. Ladies, this means we sometimes have to say no to other people clamoring for our attention, regardless of how worthy their cause!

Conforming to our husbands' preferences will also help put a stop to sinful comparisons. For instance, you should not experience guilt when your friend saves twenty dollars a week on her grocery bill by clipping coupons if your husband would rather you spend that time on other tasks than save the extra money. You shouldn't feel condemned when you see your neighbor's beautiful garden if your husband appreciates home-baked goods more than fresh bouquets of flowers.

While there is much to learn from the unique talents and abilities of other women, our goal is to more capably help our husbands—not to measure up to our friends!

So why don't we ask our husbands today how we can best help them? And let's not assume that we can ascertain their preferences through this one-time inquiry. Rather, we ought to frequently solicit their thoughts and opinions so we can manage the home to their liking.

A HAPPY MOM

As the phrase goes, "If momma ain't happy, ain't nobody happy." Poor grammar aside, there's a lot of truth in that little expression! Our attitude as home managers often determines the atmosphere and tone of the home. Therefore, we should set about our work with joy. We must seek to create an environment where our husbands, children, and others desire to be.

Scripture says that the Proverbs 31 woman (here she is again!)

"works with her hands in delight" (v. 13 NASB) and "laughs at the time to come" (v. 25). Does our laughter fill our homes, spilling over to the other members of our households? Does delight characterize the manner in which we clean the bathroom or prepare a meal?

My mother's delight in her home made a distinct impression on me as a young girl. She was always cheerful and eager to serve her family. It was not uncommon for my mom to be smiling or laughing. And I still have vivid memories of her singing hymns or praise songs as she performed her daily tasks.

I appreciated my mother's joy even more when I would spend the night with friends from school. Many of my friend's moms yelled at their children or were often unhappy and depressed. And I remember thinking, *I'm sure glad my mom's a happy mom!*

We can be sure that our husbands and children appreciate a wife and mom who does her work cheerfully. As Jean Brand puts it: "Did you know that sausages and beans taste different if the person serving them is glad to do so, or if they are hating it?"[11] No doubt our families would agree!

A HOME FOR GOD

Homemaking is a vocation often filled with mundane tasks and repetitive chores, most of which are performed in obscurity. It demands a colossal amount of serving and sacrifice. Sometimes between scrubbing toilets or laundering dirty clothes, we can lose sight of the significance of our calling. We look around us and perceive everyone engaged in meaningful work. Everyone, that is, except us. And our vision for working at home begins to flag.

What we need is a biblical perspective. For in God's economy, homemaking is a high and noble calling! Remember our ultimate mission in emulating the Titus 2 lifestyle? By "working at home" we can present the gospel as attractive to unbelievers. Our homes can actually be a showcase for the gospel!

When onlookers see us thriving in our role as homemaker, and when they observe the exceptional quality of family life that our efforts produce, this can pique their curiosity. They may want to find out what our secret is!

And our homes can be a place of momentous ministry. They are strategic locations from which we can reach out and extend care to those who don't yet know Christ.

Dawson Trotman, founder of the group called the Navigators, once said: "I believe with all my heart that one of the greatest soul saving stations in the world is the home."[12] And I love what one person observed about Dr. Francis Schaeffer's wife, Edith: "As many people were brought to the Lord through Mrs. Schaeffer's cinnamon buns as through Dr. Schaeffer's sermons!"[13]

As we realize the exceptional fruit that working at home can bear, we will be inspired to fashion an abode that rivals this lovely description from Peter Marshall, former chaplain of the Senate:

> I was privileged, in the spring, to visit in a home that was to me— and I am sure to the occupants—a little bit of Heaven. There was beauty there. There was a keen appreciation of the finer things of life, and *an atmosphere in which it was impossible to keep from thinking of God.*
>
> The room was bright and white and clean, as well as cozy. There were many windows. Flowers were blooming in pots and vases, adding their fragrance and beauty. Books lined one wall— good books—inspiring and instructive—good books—good friends. Three bird cages hung in the brightness and color of this beautiful sanctuary, and the songsters voiced their appreciation by singing as if their little throats would burst.
>
> Nature's music, nature's beauty—nature's peace. . . . It seemed to me a kind of Paradise that had wandered down, an enchanted oasis—home.[14] (emphasis mine)

What an extraordinary thought—that we can create a home where it is "impossible to keep from thinking of God."

Our houses need not resemble a page from *House Beautiful* magazine. Regardless of their size and style or our financial status, our homes can exude warmth and provide refreshment for all who walk through their doors. They should be pleasant havens for our husbands and children, sanctuaries where we offer care and hospitality to other Christians, and gateways from which we extend the gospel to family, friends, and neighbors.

So I have made this my prayer: "Lord, help me to build the kind of home where all who enter find it 'impossible to keep from thinking of God'."

Why not make this your prayer too?

THE BEST JOB IN THE WORLD

When I reflect upon my past twenty-eight years as a homemaker, a virtual collage of memories floods my mind: *Family Night every Monday. Reading with my husband by the fire. Tucking my children into bed at night with a song and a prayer. Waking them up for a surprise "pajama ride" to Dunkin' Donuts. Reading* Little House on the Prairie *to my daughters or* Paddington Bear *to my little boy.*

Counseling a newlywed couple through their first disagreement. Evenings of fellowship, food, and laughter with friends. Throwing a baby shower for my unsaved neighbor. Extending hospitality to overnight guests. Praying with other women in my living room.

Long talks with C. J. over a cup of coffee. Enjoying sweet forgiveness after resolving a family conflict. Extended family dinnertime conversations. Sharing with our children the good news of Jesus Christ.

And I'll never forget this memory: I was standing at my kitchen sink, washing the breakfast dishes when Chad entered the room. Only four years old at the time, he began running in little-boy circles in front of the refrigerator. He was singing a song he'd made up, and it went like this: "You're the best mommy in the whole world! You're the best mommy in the whole world!"

Though his song had only this one refrain, he continued singing for a full five minutes. I stood there with the dirty dishes, watching my son and thinking, *I have the BEST JOB in the whole world!*

My hope for this chapter is that as a fellow homemaker, *you* too will agree!

7

The Rewards of Kindness

❧

Entering my garage, I immediately detected a foul odor in the air, and it wasn't coming from the trashcans. The stench was spilling out of the freezer where the door hung slightly ajar. I opened it wide and was engulfed by a warm, offensive cloud. Stupefied, I gazed incredulously at the spoiled contents of my freezer.

Pans of lasagna and chicken kiev and Mason jars brimming with marinara sauce—all prepared and frozen to serve my family on busy days. Packages of boneless, skinless chicken breasts purchased at half price. Ground beef. Turkey. Steaks. Ice cream and juice. And then there was the fruit—blueberries, cherries, and blackberries I had painstakingly picked at a local farm and frozen for pies, muffins, and pancakes. Everything was thawed, mushy, and rotten.

Several hundred dollars worth of food. Innumerable hours of labor. All lost because someone had failed to close the freezer door properly. I was pretty sure I knew who the culprit was, and after a brief investigation my suspicions were confirmed.

Countless times I had warned my daughter that *slamming* the freezer door only caused it to pop open again. But had she listened? No. And now because of her recklessness all of my carefully preserved food was wasted.

I was one unhappy mom.

My daughter had already left for work, but I spent the remainder of the morning and afternoon fuming over her heedless behavior. By the time she arrived home, I had a well-rehearsed lecture prepared. Actually, it was more like an interrogation except that she never had a chance to reply. My goal was to make her feel as condemned as possible for her unforgivable crime.

KINDNESS AND GOODNESS

I'm sad to say that this episode with my daughter and the freezer was not the first nor the last time I expressed impatience or anger to a member of my immediate family. However, if on my wedding day you had informed me that I would one day display such anger against my children, I probably would have thought you were crazy. Or if you predicted that I would occasionally struggle with bitterness toward the wonderful man I was marrying, I would have laughed at you. At the very least, I would have concluded that you just didn't know me very well.

You see, I thought of myself as a compliant, easy-going individual. I hardly ever got angry. I naturally assumed that I would treat my new husband and future children with more kindness, love, and gentleness than I showed anyone else. Obviously, I was wrong.

If you are a wife and mother, I am willing to bet that you too have been shocked by the resentment or hostility you've felt (and most likely manifested) toward your own family members. Maybe you sometimes wonder, as I did: *What happened to the kind, compassionate person I used to be?*

Along with the many delights of marriage and motherhood comes a myriad of temptations to unkindness that we often do not anticipate. Thus the relevance of this command in Titus 2 for the older women to teach the younger women to be kind. No less than the other six virtues, this quality is essential for us to commend the gospel in our homes and through our lives.

In order to tease out the full meaning of the imperative to be kind, we must also address the topic of doing good. For goodness is implicit in the definition of the Greek word for "kind" in this passage.

Author Jerry Bridges explains that while *kindness* and *goodness* can often be used interchangeably, it is helpful to distinguish between these two traits. "Kindness" he says, "is a sincere *desire* for the happiness of others," and "goodness is the *activity* calculated to advance that happiness"[1] (emphasis mine).

For the purpose of this study, we will apply both of these useful definitions specifically to our relationships with our husbands and children. We will investigate three sins that hinder a sincere desire for our husbands' and children's happiness. Then we will look at five activities to advance their happiness.

Although I will make specific application for wives and mothers, I hope this chapter will encourage all women as we aspire to the lovely qualities of kindness and goodness. But before we rush ahead and try to become kind and good women, we must pause and reflect on how this is even possible.

ASK FOR HELP!

I trust in the preceding chapters I have adequately proven from Scripture that we cannot accomplish *anything* in our own strength. However, I also hope you are persuaded that God has not left us stranded by our own inability. Pastor Robert D. Jones relates the following illustration:

> The story is told of a dad who asked his young son to lift a very heavy object, a weight far beyond the little boy's capacity. The object would not budge. "Try again, son." The boy tried again with no success. "Son, you're not using all your strength." The boy tried again, but still the object would not move. "Son, you're still not using all your strength."
>
> "Oh, Daddy, Daddy, I'm trying," grunted the boy as he strained at the immovable object. "I'm using all my strength."
>
> "No, you're not, son," replied the father. "You haven't asked *me* to help!"[2]

Warning: Please do not try to lift the "heavy objects" of kindness and goodness on your own! You won't be able to do it. But our heavenly Father has provided the Holy Spirit—the Helper—to assist us (John 14:26). In fact, both kindness and goodness are the "fruit of the Spirit," says Galatians 5:22.

So let's cease straining in our own power and turn to our Helper. Let's ask Him for the strength and ability to demonstrate kindness and goodness. Our vigorous effort is still required, but it is only effective in cooperation with the Holy Spirit.

HINDRANCES TO KINDNESS

With that brief review of the Spirit's role and our responsibility, we will examine some common hindrances to kindness. Remember our working definition of kindness? It is "a sincere desire for our husbands' and children's happiness." Three sins that often obstruct this godly desire are anger, bitterness, and judging. Let's inspect these hindrances and see how to overcome them.

Hindrance #1: Anger

If we hold out a soaking wet sponge and squeeze it, what will happen? Water will fall on the floor. We may look at the puddle and think it was caused by the squeeze. However, the squeeze only revealed what was already in the sponge. You could squeeze a dry sponge, but no water would come out.

What's the point?

As with a sponge, what is in our hearts will spill out of us when the squeeze is on. In other words, difficult interactions or trying experiences (the squeeze perpetrators) are not the *cause* of our angry reactions; rather they serve to *reveal* the sin that was there all along.[3] Matthew 15:18 says that "what comes out of the mouth proceeds from the heart."

Expressions of anger reveal sinful desires in our hearts, cravings that are not being satisfied. Dr. David Powlison offers this description of sinful anger: "I want my way and not God's, and because I can't have my way, I rage."[4] As it says in James 4:1-2, "What causes quarrels and what causes fights among you? Is it not this, that your passions are at war within you? You desire and do not have."

So what do I want that I'm not getting? Am I craving peace and quiet, convenience and ease, a clean and orderly house, appreciation and recognition? Or do I long to get even, inflict hurt, be right, win the argument? Whatever it is, we need to recognize that "wanting my way" is really the driving force that propels our anger.

A sinful desire for my own way was the source of my anger in the freezer illustration at the beginning of the chapter. My anger wasn't caused by the squeeze—my daughter leaving the freezer door open. Her actions only exposed a reservoir of sinful demands in my heart: *I have a right to benefit from the bounty of my freezer. I deserve to reap the fruit of all my labors. I do not want to have to restock the freezer. I definitely do not want to clean it out. And most of all, I hope my daughter feels very guilty!* You may think that these desires don't sound all that bad. They may seem entirely reasonable. But as Dr. Powlison (paraphrasing John Calvin) articulates: "The evil in our desires often lies not in what we want but that we want it too much."[5] My problem was that I wanted these desires satisfied *more* than I wanted to glorify God by being kind.

Scripture's Solution to Anger

After a straightforward diagnosis of our anger, James 4 prescribes the remedy: We must humble ourselves and submit to God (vv. 6-10). When we are tempted to sinful anger, we must ask the Holy Spirit to open our spiritual eyes to perceive the sinfulness of our cravings.

It is helpful to ask the question: "What do I want *more* than I want to please God?" Then we must confess and repent from these evil desires. This requires humility, but we have God's pledge that He will give grace to the humble (James 4:6). He will help us turn from anger and cultivate kindness.

Hindrance #2: Bitterness

None of us should presume to be impervious to the sin of bitterness. Author Jim Wilson explains the nature of this particular temptation:

> Bitterness is based on sin that somehow relates to you. It is not concerned with how big the sin is; it is based upon how close it is. For instance, if some great and gross immorality occurs in [another country], what do we do? . . . We might be appalled or amazed, but . . . we do not feel bitter. Nevertheless, it was an awful sin, and someone actually committed it. So it does not depend on how great the evil is; *it depends on how close the other person is to me.* . . .
>
> Who are likely candidates? The answer is simple: fathers, mothers, brothers, sisters, husbands, wives, children . . . roommates . . . co-workers . . . and . . . other relatives. . . . There are even many people who are bitter against God.
>
> . . . Bitterness is based upon somebody else's sin who is close to us, and who did something to us. It might be minor. It does not have to be great; *it just has to be close.* Does he pick up his socks?

No? Can you get bitter over that? Well, no, but what if he does it 5,000 times?

You may think you have a right to be bitter. But the Bible does not grant anyone the right to be bitter. [Eph. 4:31] says *to get rid of all bitterness.*[6]

As wives and mothers, we must be especially wary of developing bitterness toward our husbands and children—our closest relationships. For they will surely wrong us in small ways and maybe even significant ways. Because of sin, they will say and do things that inflict pain. In these moments we must be on our guard against bitterness.

We should not be duped into thinking that we merely suffer from a case of "hurt feelings." While "hurt feelings" aren't equivalent to bitterness, they usually don't remain "hurt feelings" for very long. They can rapidly metamorphose into bitterness.

So how do we know if we have become bitter? If we habitually review the offender's wrong, if we replay the episode over and over in our minds, if we wallow in self-pity or withdraw our affection—chances are we have succumbed to bitterness. And we cannot pursue a sincere desire for our families' happiness when bitterness blocks the way.

Scripture's Solution to Bitterness

To knock down the barricade of bitterness, we must heed the instructions in Ephesians 4:31-32: "Let all bitterness . . . be put away from you. . . . Be kind to one another, tenderhearted, forgiving one another, *as God in Christ forgave you*" (emphasis mine).

We deal with bitterness by cherishing the experience of being forgiven by God and by forgiving the wrongs committed against us. In his book *The Cross-Centered Life*, my husband makes the following observation:

> When I become bitter or unforgiving toward others, I'm assuming that the sins of others are more serious than my sins against God. The cross transforms my perspective. Through the cross I realize that no sin committed against me will ever be as serious as the innumerable sins I've committed against God. When we understand how much God has forgiven us, it's not difficult to forgive others.[7]

So instead of dwelling on how we've been wronged, let us entreat the Holy Spirit to help us look at the cross. As we meditate on the undeserved mercy of God in forgiving our sins, we will freely grant forgiveness and kindness to our husbands and children.

Hindrance #3: Judging

Several years ago I came across this comical poem:

> *A woman was waiting at an airport one night,*
> *With several long hours before her flight.*
> *She hunted for a book in the airport shop,*
> *Bought a bag of cookies and found a place to drop.*
> *She was engrossed in her book, but happened to see,*
> *That the man sitting beside her, as bold as could be,*
> *Grabbed a cookie or two from the bag between,*
> *Which she tried to ignore, to avoid a scene.*
> *She read, munched cookies, and watched the clock,*
> *As the gutsy "cookie thief" diminished her stock.*
> *She was getting more irritated as the minutes ticked by,*
> *Thinking, If I wasn't so nice, I would blacken his eye!*
> *With each cookie she took, he took one too.*
> *When only one was left, she wondered what he'd do.*
> *With a smile on his face and a nervous laugh,*
> *He took the last cookie and broke it in half.*
> *He offered her half, as he ate the other.*
> *She snatched it from him and thought, Oh brother,*
> *This guy has some nerve and he's also rude.*
> *Why, he didn't even show any gratitude!*
> *She had never known when she had been so galled,*
> *And sighed with relief when her flight was called.*
> *She gathered her belongings and headed to the gate,*
> *Refusing to look back at the "thieving ingrate."*
> *She boarded the plane and sank in her seat,*
> *Then sought her book, which was almost complete.*
> *As she reached in her baggage, she gasped*
>   *with surprise:*
> *There were her cookies in front of her eyes.*
> *If mine are here, she moaned with despair,*
> *Then the others were his and he tried to share!*
> *Too late to apologize, she realized with grief,*
> *That she was the rude one, the ingrate, the thief!*[8]

Much to my chagrin, I can relate to this poor woman. I have frequently made negative assumptions about others only to discover later that I was the one in the wrong. The Bible calls this judging. Because of remaining sin, we all have a propensity to engage in this evil activity.

Author and teacher Ken Sande defines judging as "looking for others' faults and, without valid and sufficient reason, forming unfavorable opinions of their qualities, words, actions, or motives. In simple terms, it means *looking for the worst in others*."[9] As with anger and bitterness, we are most inclined to "look for the worst" in those closest to us. Such is often the case with me.

For example, one morning my husband called me from work and asked me to reschedule a meeting I had arranged with a neighbor that day. Not at all happy about this modification, I proceeded to judge his motives: *He's only thinking about how this change will serve him. He's not concerned about how it messes up my plans!*

Well, imagine my shame and remorse when only an hour later several dear friends arrived at my door and announced that they were taking me on a surprise outing. I now understood that C. J.'s actions were actually intended to bless me. Yet I had not hesitated to attribute evil motives to his behavior.

Scripture instructs us: "Do not judge by appearances, but judge with right judgment" (John 7:24). Sinful judging can wreak havoc with the desire for our husbands' and children's happiness; therefore, we must be vigilant in our efforts to resist this temptation.

Scripture's Solution to Judging

Instead of persistently looking for faults in our family members, we must enlist the Holy Spirit's aid to make loving judgments. We should think the best that the nature of a case will allow, placing the best possible construction on their words, actions, and motives.

First Corinthians 13:7 says, "Love bears all things, believes all things, hopes all things, endures all things." If we become conscious of believing the worst about our husbands and children, we must confess our lack of love for them to God. When we repent from judging, we will gain fresh passion for our families' happiness.

Now exercising loving judgments does not mean that we ignore sin in the lives of family members. Rather, we are not to *presume* that they are sinning unless there is solid evidence. If there are clear indications that a family member is sinning in a manner too serious to overlook, we must humbly approach the person and *ask* if we perceive the situation accurately. We should never *assume* that we know or *accuse* before we know. If correction is necessary, we should bring it with all humility and kindness.

GRACE CONQUERS SIN

I recently saw a Family Circus cartoon that showed three children leaning on the edge of their parents' bed, watching them while they slept. The caption underneath was one child's remark: "They look so sweet and peaceful when they're asleep. You wonder how they could ever yell at us during the day."[10]

Do you ever wonder if this scenario is taking place in your home? Do you have a sneaking suspicion that your husband or children sometimes watch you sleep and marvel at how kind and peaceful you appear compared to when you are awake?

While we should all aggressively seek to remove the hindrances of anger, bitterness, and judging, we will likely fail at times to be kind. On the heels of our failure can come a fear that we have caused irreparable damage to our family relationships.

Yet this fear leaves God out of the picture. Although it is true that we have the potential to inflict harm on family members, the grace of God can still bring forth good, even out of our sin. Romans 8:28 tells us, "And we know that for those who love God *all things* work together for good, for those who are called according to his purpose" (emphasis mine). That means, no situation created by our sin is so horrible that God can't redeem it for good—both for us and for our families.

This brought me hope after an occasion when I was unkind toward one of my daughters. Though I had repented before God and asked my daughter's forgiveness, I still felt terrible! I berated myself for treating my child in such a manner.

But my husband imparted some Romans 8:28 encouragement to me: "Because of your humility in asking her to forgive you, she feels closer to you now than before." And he was right! This daughter and I were enjoying the sweet closeness that follows repentance in a relationship.

Now I'm not issuing a free pass to sin! I am *not* saying, "It's okay to be unkind to your children or husband. They're tough. They can handle it." Sin is *always* the wrong choice. It does have consequences. So by the Holy Spirit, we must work tirelessly to eradicate it from our lives (Rom. 8:13).

When we are unkind to our husbands or children, we should not make excuses for ourselves. We must confess our sin to God and humbly ask our family members for their forgiveness. However, let us find hope in God's grace, which both covers the offense of our sin and works it for good.

A REPUTATION FOR GOODNESS

Now that we are well on our way to identifying sins that hinder a sincere desire for our husbands' and children's happiness, let's talk about putting that desire into action. This brings us to goodness—the *activity* calculated to advance our families' happiness.

We'll begin by playing a little game. I have listed below the names of six well-known women from recent history to the present day. Read each name on the list and then jot down one word that best describes your perception of that person's character.

Princess Diana
Hillary Clinton
Corrie Ten Boom
Elizabeth Taylor
Harriet Tubman
Brittany Spears

Take a look at the words you used to describe each of these women. Whether your depiction was favorable or unfavorable, the common feature is that all of them have a reputation. Though we may never have given it much thought, so do we!

Furthermore, Scripture has defined what *our* reputation is to be. It says that we are to be known for our good works. First Timothy 2:9-10 explicates, "women should adorn themselves in respectable apparel, with modesty and self-control, not with braided hair and gold or pearls or costly attire, *but with what is proper for women who profess godliness—with good works*" (emphasis mine).

Again in 1 Timothy 5:9 it says, "Let a widow be enrolled if she is not less than sixty years of age, having been the wife of one husband, and *having a reputation for good works*: if she has brought up children, has shown hospitality, has washed the feet of the saints, has cared for the afflicted, and *has devoted herself to every good work*" (emphasis mine).

What are *we* known for? How would our family and friends portray our character? As these people observe our lives, they should be more aware of our good deeds than our style of clothing, our talents and abilities, our hobbies, or our standard of living. We should be renowned for good works at home, in our churches, and extending into our communities. Of course, the goal is not to garner attention for ourselves, but to show forth the compelling power of the gospel.

Let's not forget, however, that this reputation for goodness *begins* at home. At the heart of our commission to do good is the well-being of our family members. Our husbands and children should be the primary beneficiaries of our good works.

While there are countless avenues of goodness we can pursue for our families' joy, we will survey only five in the remainder of this chapter. But each one is a vital expression of goodness. We should be women who are known for praying, greeting, listening, encouraging, and planning.

Renown for Praying

"The prayer of a righteous man is powerful and effective," says James 5:16 (NIV). This text goes on to tell the story of Elijah and what happened when he prayed: "Elijah was a man just like us. He prayed earnestly that it would not rain, and it did not rain on the land for three and a half years. Again he prayed, and the heavens gave rain, and the earth produced its crops" (vv. 17-18).

James notes that Elijah was "just like us." He was an ordinary human being, possessing no mystical powers or special abilities. Yet his prayers produced phenomenal results: It didn't rain for over three years!

What spectacular potential prayer has to further our husbands' and children's happiness! And who better to pray for them than us? No one knows our family members the way we do. No one is more familiar with the unique temptations and pressures they face. No one can pray for them with keener insight or greater compassion.

Therefore, we should be committed to the "good work" of praying for our husbands and children. And what's more, we should *inform* them of our prayers. For what could be more encouraging to the members of our families than having wives or mothers who faithfully intercede? As Charles Spurgeon once said: "No man can do me a truer kindness in this world than to pray for me."[11]

Renown for Greeting

Suppose you answer a knock at your door only to discover—the Prize Patrol. Happy people with balloons, flowers, a video camera, and a very large check. How would you greet them? Would you listlessly mutter, "Oh, hi," and then walk away from the door? Of course not! After recovering from the shock, you would eagerly invite them into your home and extend every effort to make them feel welcome!

So how do we greet our husbands when they arrive home from work each evening? What kind of welcome can our children expect when they walk through the door after school or play? Do we receive them with the same exuberance we would a member of the Prize Patrol? Certainly our families are worth far more to us than a million dollar check!

It's easy to miss, but Scripture is actually laden with commands and examples of greeting. Open to almost any epistle in the New Testament, and you will observe the apostles urging the believers to greet one another or sending greetings themselves (Rom. 16:16; Titus 3:15; 1 Peter 5:14; 3 John 14, just to name a few instances).

Our lives should mirror Scripture's pattern, and—you guessed it—as wives and mothers, our family members should be the recipients of our most enthusiastic greetings. When they awake each morning, call on the telephone, or enter the house, this seemingly small act of greeting will go a long way to advance their happiness.

Renown for Listening

I realized a change was needed when my son Chad began to preface his questions with, "Mom, before you give me an answer, please listen to the whole thing!" Apparently, I was not excelling at listening. Being an attentive listener is an essential "good work" for any wife and mother.

A mother is usually the person that every member of the family wants to talk to—occasionally all at the same time! On some days we might wish for a headset that completely blocks out all the questions, stories, and comments. Yet taking a sincere interest in what our husbands and children desire to communicate is a primary way to bring them joy.

Listening is more than just keeping our mouths shut. It means making full eye contact, not looking around with a blank stare. It is not interrupting, yawning, or prematurely formulating an answer. Attentive listening entails an eagerness to hear *everything* with regard to our families' thoughts, feelings, and experiences.

Careful listening will encourage our husbands to bare their souls to us. It will motivate our children to share their innermost thoughts. As Proverbs 20:5 observes: "The purpose in a man's heart is like deep water, but a man of understanding will draw it out." Listening is the prerequisite to being a "woman of understanding" who draws out "deep water" from the hearts of her family members. So may our husbands and children know that we want to hear all about it!

Renown for Encouraging

The woman seated next to me on the plane was addressing envelopes. As we struck up a conversation, I discovered that she was sending out graduation invitations for one daughter and wedding invitations for the other. I was about to congratulate her when she quipped, "It's so nice to be getting rid of both of them at the same time." I silently cringed and thought to myself, *I'm sure glad her daughters didn't hear that comment!*

What if our family members overheard us talking about them to another person? What would they hear? Or in speaking directly *to* them—what kind of words do we communicate? Proverbs 12:25 says that "a good word makes [a husband or child] glad." We should be lavish in our dispersal of "good words" to and about our families.

Daily we should bestow much more encouragement than correction or criticism. We should be on the lookout for praiseworthy actions that glorify God and point out these evidences of grace to our husbands and children. *Specific* encouragement of this kind will strengthen their souls and provoke them to godliness.

Let's also seize opportunities to compliment our husbands and children when talking to others—in their presence, if possible! We want to foster the reputation of being women who shower their families with encouragement. For our good words will supply them much gladness.

Renown for Planning

A key component of our definition of goodness—the activity calculated to advance our husbands' and children's happiness—is expressed in the word *calculated*. This word implies a deliberateness and intentionality in our pursuit of goodness. For in order to achieve a reputation for good works, we must *plan* good works.

One aspect of planning involves devising solutions to anticipated problems. Though it is impossible to foresee every hardship that will come our way, we can expect certain troubles—PMS, the holiday shopping crunch, chaotic school mornings, or that one recurring conflict with our husbands.

Proverbs 22:3 advises, "The prudent sees danger and hides himself, but the simple go on and suffer for it." Planning is a method of "hiding" ourselves and our families from trouble. Yet so often we "go on" with our lives without stopping to plan. As a result we reap the same consequences over and over again.

But what if we scheduled our Christmas shopping in July or set the alarm for half an hour earlier each school morning? What if we arranged to take a nap when feeling PMS symptoms or infused our minds with Scripture before conversing with our husbands? Imagine the trouble we would spare our families and the peace and harmony that our planning would create.

Planning is not only necessary for heading off danger but also for initiating good. Good works don't just happen. We need to plan and prepare for them. And I must say, this type of planning is a whole lot of fun! It is with great glee that I seek to invent ways to bring my family happiness.

Periodically, I take time just to think about each member of my family—what that person likes and appreciates, what would entertain or refresh him or her. I might plan something as elaborate as a surprise overnight for my husband or as simple as baking my son's favorite dessert. I research options for family outings, organize weekly "girls' time out," and strategize to create special memories from ordinary activities.

Planning in advance allows me to make good on my intentions, and my family's pleasure makes it well worth the effort. Proverbs 21:5 guarantees: "The plans of the diligent lead surely to abundance." I know we all desire an abundance of happiness for our families; so let's get on with the good work of planning!

ANTICIPATING THE REWARDS

When my son was three years old, he gave me the following card for Valentine's Day:

Outside:
"Happy Valentine's Day, Mom! How 'bout breakfast in bed?"
Inside:
"Just bring it on up! Not too early, though, OK?
(And no pulp in the juice. Thanks.)"

Of course, C. J. helped Chad pick out this card. It typified my son's attitude at the time, which was: Mom exists to serve me! Since then we have endeavored to reorient his selfish thinking. But his card illustrates the reality that as wives and mothers, our labors of kindness and goodness are sometimes taken for granted.

While we may not serve it in bed each morning, we do prepare thousands of breakfasts in our lifetime. Each and every day we cheerfully welcome our family members home. We listen with rapt attention to the same story—over and over again. We bring countless prayers and burdens before God's throne. We refrain from anger, even in the face of repeated wrongs. We reserve judgment once more. We plan a myriad of special memories. Faithfully we encourage, constantly we support, and above and beyond we forgive, "seventy times seven" (Matt. 18:22).

We work tirelessly to enrich our husbands' and children's lives, and yet our toil at times goes unappreciated. We may wonder if our families even notice our efforts of kindness and goodness. However, Proverbs 31 anticipates that for the godly woman, "Her children *rise up* and call her blessed; her husband also, and he praises her: 'Many women have done excellently, but you surpass them all'" (Prov. 31:28-29, emphasis mine).

I can tell you from experience that if you devote your life to advancing your family's happiness, *the rewards will far exceed the sacrifices*. It may be awhile yet before you receive many of your rewards, but being kind and doing good *today* will yield sweet fruit in the latter years of your life. Marriage will become more precious. Motherhood will grow more dear. The rewards will start coming—with bigger and bigger returns.

However, our greatest returns are still to come, and they will far surpass what we can fathom here on earth. Ephesians 6:8 (NIV) promises, "the Lord will reward everyone for *whatever good* he does" (emphasis mine). As John Bunyan elaborates: "Whatever good thing you do for him, if done according to the Word, is laid up for you as treasure in chests and coffers, to be brought out to be rewarded before both men and angels, to your eternal comfort."[12]

So regardless of who takes notice in this life, God is watching. He is recording every expression of kindness and every act of goodness. What greater incentive could there be to advance our families' happiness?

8

The Beauty of Submission

🌹

Carol personified the modern career woman. Divorced and single, she was the only woman among eight men in a high-level sales position for a major American corporation. Her responsibilities included oversight of a ten million dollar annual sales budget. She was competent, aggressive, and in charge. In her words: "The world was right in front of me."

In her late thirties she met and fell in love with Howard, and after living together for a year, they decided to get married. By Carol's estimation, she and Howard had a great relationship. Their marriage was "based on mutuality." They both worked and made good salaries. They shared equally in household chores. Howard, who helped run his family's business, was supportive of Carol's career. He always encouraged her to go after the sale, the bonus, or the raise. "We're working together," he would cheer her on. "Go get 'em, Carol!"

But when Carol started attending church with her neighbor Diane, she observed marriages that squarely collided with her worldly understanding. What's more, she found herself curiously attracted to whatever it was that made these couples so different.

AN EXTRAORDINARY PRODUCT

At Diane's church, Carol saw husbands and wives who appeared happy to be there and happy to be there *together*. She perceived genuine love and affection in their marriages.

From the pulpit she heard biblical teaching on manhood and womanhood. She learned that men and women have equal value in the eyes of God, and she began to admire the divine wisdom of complementary roles in marriage.

As Carol visited one of the small groups and formed friendships with the women, she watched them willingly submit to their husbands' leadership. She was struck by the peace and joy that this submission produced, and she was amazed by the way these women talked about their husbands—always with honor and respect. This attitude was in stark contrast to that of her other friends, who relished their men-bashing sessions.

Soon Carol found herself longing for a marriage like the ones she was observing. "I am a saleswoman," she explained, "and I appreciate a product that works. When I went to church, I saw hundreds of women whose lives were a testament to the product of submission. *I saw that the product worked, and I wanted that for my marriage."*

In this chapter, I want to tell you more about this product. I hope to give you a biblical sales pitch, if you will, for the doctrine of submission. The specific instruction in Titus 2 is for wives to be "submissive to their own husbands." This word *submissive* in the Greek means to "voluntarily place oneself under." God has ordained our husbands' authority, and here Scripture requires us to place ourselves under their leadership.

Now I am aware that this final virtue in our list is certainly the most controversial. Not only does it radically oppose the modern worldview, but it is also the subject of vigorous debate within the church. The viewpoints are as diverse as they are impassioned.

So let me ask, "How do *you* view submission? Do you find it appealing as Carol did? Or do you cringe at the mere mention of the word?" If you react negatively to the idea, chances are you have only seen a warped or defective product, because the genuine article of submission brings immeasurable benefit to our marriages and tremendous honor to the gospel. Therefore, may I entreat you to keep reading to discover what the Bible has to say about submission in marriage? I think you might be pleasantly surprised.

I want to mention that although I will direct my thoughts to married women, I believe this subject is pertinent for those who are single as well. For Scripture conceives of submission in other relationships besides marriage—be it to employers, pastors, or civil government. While submission takes different forms in these relationships, many of the principles still hold true. Additionally, a clear understanding of submission will equip you to counsel your married friends and prepare you for marriage, should that be in your future.

EQUAL IN VALUE AND DIGNITY

So why don't we get started! Let's look at Genesis 1:27, reading it carefully: "So God created man in his own image, in the image of God he created him; male and female he created them."

What do we learn from this verse? Here we find that *both* male and female are created in the image of God. In this first chapter of the first book of the Bible, God establishes that man and woman are equal in value and dignity in His sight. A conviction of our equal worth is essential to understanding submission in the context of the marriage relationship.

Scripture makes no allowance for male dominance or male superiority. For this reason, theologian Wayne Grudem appeals, "To all societies and cultures where these abuses occur, we must proclaim that the very first page of God's Word bears a fundamental and irrefutable witness against the evil of thinking of men as better than women."[1]

Neither is submission a position of inferiority or demeaning in its application. For although God has designed men and women to fulfill differing roles, He unequivocally affirms that they are equal in worth and importance. As it says in 1 Peter 3:7, husbands and wives are heirs *together* of the grace of life.

WHOSE IDEA WAS THIS ANYWAY?

Believe it or not, wifely submission was not a conspiracy concocted over the centuries by power-hungry men. It was not a result of the Fall or because Paul and Peter were chauvinists. It wasn't even your husband's idea! *Submission originated with God.* In fact, we see submission represented in the very character of God. As Dr. Grudem elaborates:

> The idea of headship and submission never began! It has *always* *existed* in the eternal nature of God Himself. And in this most basic

of all authority relationships, authority is not based on gifts or ability; it is just there. . . . [The relationship between the Father, Son, and Holy Spirit] is one of leadership and authority on the one hand and voluntary, willing, joyful submission to that authority on the other hand. We can learn from this that submission to a rightful authority is a noble virtue. It is a privilege. It is something good and desirable. It is the virtue that has been demonstrated by the eternal Son of God *forever*. It is His glory, the glory of the Son as He relates to His Father.[2]

To further display this glory, God instituted a husband's leadership and a wife's submission at the beginning of creation, prior to the entrance of sin (Gen. 1—3). The Lord restates His divine order for marriage all through the pages of Scripture. In every New Testament passage that addresses the role of the wife to the husband, we find this edict for wives to submit (Eph. 5:22-24; Col. 3:18; Titus 2:5; 1 Peter 3:1-5).

Then God reveals His ultimate intention for headship and submission in marriage: It is to reflect the relationship of Christ and the church (Eph. 5:22-33). The husband is to mirror the sacrificial love of Christ by laying down his life for his wife, and the wife is to exemplify the church's joyful submission to Christ by following her husband's leadership.

So do you see now that the concept of submission originated in the gracious heart of *God*? This command is not punishment for our sin. Neither is it optional or devised by man. Rather, it is *God* who determined that we are to voluntarily place ourselves under our husbands' authority. He designed submission for *His* glory.

(God's plan for complementary roles in marriage is a vast subject, and I have only scratched the surface in these few paragraphs. If you are interested in further study, I recommend *Recovering Biblical Manhood and Womanhood*, edited by John Piper and Wayne Grudem and published by Crossway Books. In my opinion this collection of essays is the most biblical and comprehensive resource available on the topic today.)

THE TROUBLE WITH SUBMISSION

Elisabeth Elliot made this comment about Ephesians 5:22 ("Wives, submit to your own husbands, as to the Lord"):

Many are the discussions I've heard on this one, almost all of them directed to what it "can't possibly mean," rather than to the plain word of the Lord. The statement is simple. Not easy for women like me, but *simple*, that is, I understand it only too well. (As Mark Twain said, "I have far more trouble with the things I *do* understand in the Bible than things I don't understand.")[3]

Why do we have trouble with the practice of submission? What is it about this command that can make us bristle? Even though we may accept, as Elisabeth Elliot does, the clarity of Scripture on the issue, we also can agree that submitting to our husbands is not always easy.

Certainly our culture presents us with a formidable challenge. It treats the submissive wife with a noxious mixture of scorn and pity. And it doesn't help that many in the church are trying to explain away this command, thus cutting off a vital source of our encouragement.

But the real threat to submission originates in a place we may not initially suspect—our very own hearts! My good friend Marianne confronted this reality shortly after her marriage to her husband, Kevin. See if you can relate, as I did, to her account:

> The whole idea of submission was a real challenge for me. I knew what Scripture said in Titus, Ephesians, and 1 Peter—I just didn't like those parts very much! You see, I was raised to be very independent. I was strong and self-sufficient. I thought I was capable of taking care of myself and doing a pretty good job of it. I didn't like being led. I liked leading. This was especially true when it came to my schedule and how I spent money. And because I wanted to make decisions about these things on my own, Kevin and I had some heated conflicts! I made it very difficult for my husband to lead.

Scripture sheds light on this struggle to submit—for Marianne and for the rest of us! One of the consequences of the Fall for women, it says in Genesis 3:16, is that their "desire shall be for [their] husband[s]."

The form and context of the word *desire* actually has a negative connotation—an urge to manipulate, control, or have mastery over. Because of the curse, we now have a sinful tendency to want our own way and to resist our husbands' authority. This evil desire poses the greatest opposition to our submission.

So we see that the submissive wife—far from being the weak-willed woman our culture portrays—is actually a model of inner strength. By God's grace, she has conquered this opposition within her own heart. It is actually weakness on display when a wife is not submissive; she is only caving in to her natural inclination to usurp authority and demand her own way. That doesn't take any effort at all!

This truth eventually dawned upon Marianne. When she realized that her adversary was not her husband, Kevin, but the sin in her heart, she began fighting back—by submitting to his leadership. The result was peace and joy for Marianne and a newfound harmony in her relationship with her husband.

Now, some twenty years later, Marianne freely admits that submission is still a struggle at times. However, her thriving marriage testifies of her persistent efforts to resist sin and follow her husband's leadership.

A SUBMISSION TOUR

In order to probe our Titus 2 charge more extensively, I would like to invite you on a little tour. We will follow one of Scripture's most penetrating passages on this topic of wives submitting to their husbands—1 Peter 3:1-6. Through these verses, we will peer into the character and impact of submission. Along the way, we will uncover the source of hope for attaining this virtue. We will conclude by meeting an unlikely role model of wifely submission. Let's begin by reading the passage in its entirety:

> [1]*Likewise, wives, be subject to your own husbands, so that even if some do not obey the word, they may be won without a word by the conduct of their wives—*
>
> [2]*when they see your respectful and pure conduct.*
>
> [3]*Do not let your adorning be external—the braiding of hair, the wearing of gold, or the putting on of clothing—*
>
> [4]*but let your adorning be the hidden person of the heart with the imperishable beauty of a gentle and quiet spirit, which in God's sight is very precious.*

⁵*For this is how the holy women who hoped in God used to adorn themselves, by submitting to their husbands,*

⁶*as Sarah obeyed Abraham, calling him lord. And you are her children, if you do good and do not fear anything that is frightening.*

JUST TO CLARIFY

The first stop on our tour is verse 1: "Likewise, wives, be subject to your own husbands." It is critical that we pause here to consider two points of clarification.

First of all, note to whom this command is addressed: to *wives*. Submission was not our husbands' idea, and neither are they responsible to enforce it. This command is *not* divine permission for husbands to assert authoritarian leadership. Nowhere in Scripture does it say, "Husbands, see to it that your wives submit."

The requirement to submit to our husbands comes straight from God, to us as wives. And we are answerable to *Him* for our obedience. We cannot blame our husbands for our lack of submission. The responsibility is entirely ours!

Secondly, we ascertain to whom we are to submit. As married women, we are not to submit to *all* men, but rather to our husbands. Conversely, we should not seek leadership from *other* men, apart from our husbands, no matter how worthy they are of honor or respect. We are to be subject to *our own* husbands.

A SUITABLE HELPER

Let's focus for a minute on those two little words, "be subject." If to you they represent brainless obedience or servile status, then think again. Being subject is an altogether honorable role that calls forth the full measure of our energy, ability, and godly character. For as we see in Genesis 2:20, woman was called to be man's *helpmate*, not his *helpless mate*.

John Piper presents wifely submission as "the divine calling to honor and affirm her husband's leadership and help carry it through according to her gifts."⁴ God has graced each of us with unique gifts that He intends for us to use to support our husbands. We are to contribute our ideas and suggestions, offer wisdom and insight, pray and encourage, as well as correct. When we carry out these acts of service in all humility, we help our husbands to lead and fulfill our biblical duty to submit.

Katharine Luther, wife of reformer Martin Luther, was a model of helpful submission. She was not bashful in her communication with her husband. Although respectful, she pointedly and sometimes humorously furnished him with counsel.

On one occasion when Martin was extremely depressed and indifferent to encouragement, Katharine donned mourning attire. Her husband asked her, "Katharine, why are you dressed in mourning black?"

"Someone has died," she replied.

"Died?" said Luther. "I have not heard of anyone dying. Whoever can have died?"

"It seems," his wife replied, "that God must have died!"[5]

By her clever confrontation, Katharine exhorted her husband to repent from his sin and renew his trust in God. She is truly a helper worth emulating!

But as submissive wives, we must also bear in mind that our husbands have the authority to lead and make final decisions. We are to give our advice, for sure. However, when a conflict of opinion arises that cannot be resolved, they are responsible to decide, and we are responsible to "honor and affirm their leadership."

EXCUSES AND EXCEPTIONS

By now some of you may be asking, "What about submission in my case? Surely God doesn't expect me to submit to *my* husband!"

Not surprisingly, Scripture anticipates that question. While our 1 Peter text does not fail to offer hope to women in difficult marriages, verse 1 clearly stipulates that wives are to submit to their husbands "even if some do not obey the word."

"But," you may contend, "my husband is lazy and inconsiderate."

"All my husband ever does is watch ESPN."

"My husband is irresponsible with the finances."

"I have a husband who never disciplines the children."

"I am married to a man who doesn't lead our family well."

"My husband isn't a Christian."

However, none of these excuses is admissible. Unless a moral issue is at stake, we are obliged by Scripture to submit to our husbands. As Elisabeth Elliot bluntly states, God's Word does not "give us any footnotes."[6]

Of course, we must never follow our husbands' leadership into sin. For while their authority is genuine, it is by no means absolute. Our preeminent authority is God Himself, and at no time should our submission violate any of His expressed commands (Acts 5:29).

Also, if we observe a sin pattern in our husbands that we deem detrimental to our families, but our husbands do not agree—we must make an appeal. We should ask our husbands if together we can obtain counsel from a pastor or godly couple.

I have met women who incorrectly interpreted submission to mean: "I follow my husband regardless of the consequences to my family." But this does not characterize a helpmate in the truest sense of the word. Requesting assistance in such circumstances *is* helping our husbands.

Having said all this, you may still be uncertain how to respond in a godly manner to your unique situation. If so, I would like to suggest Ken Sande's book *The Peacemaker* (Baker Book House). The biblical principles of conflict resolution presented in this manual will provide invaluable counsel and guidance.

THE POWER OF SUBMISSION

Submission is not a static character quality. It is a powerful, dynamic force that can actually influence an unbelieving husband! Look again at verse 1: "Likewise, wives, be subject to your own husbands, so that even if some do not obey the word, *they may be won without a word by the conduct of their wives*" (emphasis mine).

Here we will resume Carol's story from the beginning of our chapter. After attending church with her friend Diane, Carol eventually put her trust in Jesus Christ. But Carol's husband, Howard, although happy for Carol, was more interested in his weekend recreation than in going to church. However, Carol grasped the truth of 1 Peter 3:1. She believed her godly conduct would affect Howard more than any words she might say.

When I gave my life to the Lord, it was a huge change. This was the greatest thing that had ever happened to me. But I knew I could not force my experience on Howard. I couldn't coerce him or make him change. This was so different from my sales background of taking control, manipulating, doing things in my own time and in my own way. I had to retrain myself and let the Lord work in Howard's heart. I had to be *very* patient. And I knew change needed to start with me.

I saw God's plan for us as wives. We are to be our husbands' helpers. So I began to let Howard lead. I had to acquiesce and do things differently. I learned to have faith in God, and as I submitted to the Lord, submitting to my husband became much easier.

I began to say things like, "Howard, whatever you decide," or "You can make that decision." I stopped overreacting when we had challenges or putting pressure on him to come up with the answers. I would just tell him that I would be praying about it, and I was fine with whatever happened.

While we used to share domestic responsibilities, I now took charge of the home. I tried to make it a warm haven for Howard. When he came home, instead of a list of chores waiting for him, he didn't have anything to do. I found a lot of joy in taking care of the house and not burdening him with additional responsibilities.

There used to be bitterness and tension when Howard would go out fishing, golfing, or skiing. But now I began to freely release him. I knew I couldn't just grit my teeth and say, "Have a good time" and seethe as he went out the door. I really had to have joy in my heart that he was having a good time. And the more I released him to do the things he wanted to do, the more joy I had.

I also began loving on my husband. I would write him notes and leave them on the bathroom mirror or on the car windshield. I went overboard on loving him! My non-Christian friends were like, "What is up with you, Carol, warming up his car in the morning and letting him go out all day on weekends?"

But I knew that I could turn to God whenever bitterness crept in. I also knew that I could call my friend Diane. "Carol," she would remind me, "trust in the Lord. Remember, *be joyful*." Diane would always refer me to Scripture. The women in my small group were also praying for me and setting an example for me to follow.

And every night I would pray. I wanted my husband to know the Lord. Yes, there was anxiety. I was anxious for the Lord to intervene. But I was learning to trust Him. I prayed and I prayed, and God heard.

Carol's submissive conduct began to prompt change in Howard's life:

> Howard didn't say anything, but he started changing. He saw a peace in me, and he became more relaxed. And because I was releasing him, he became more apt to stay home or come home early from playing golf.

As Carol patiently waited, God softened Howard's heart. He started visiting church with Carol, and almost four years later, he repented and believed. Carol now marvels at the transformation in Howard's life:

> Today Howard loves and trusts in God, and he is very involved in the church. He is on the take-down crew, the sound crew, and leads worship for our small group. He is in a Bible study with one of the pastors. At home the change has also been dramatic. Howard has stepped up to the plate. He is the leader of our household. He makes decisions based on what is best for our family, and he is not afraid to do it. We truly serve a faithful God, and I am convinced that He hears our prayers. He will answer in *His* time.

What a remarkable testimony! And I hope it did not escape your notice—here is another striking example of true *feminine appeal*. The virtue of submission—along with the other six virtues—brilliantly displays the gospel.

As Diane and the women in her church modeled the quality of submission, the beauty of their lives captured Carol's attention. She was compelled to discover the reason for their joy, and she encountered the gospel.

When Carol undertook the pursuit of a submissive heart, Howard, in turn, was intrigued. And God used Carol's obedience to draw Howard to Himself.

What power is in these virtues to affect souls for eternity!

APPLYING GODLY PRESSURE

Now if submission can have such profound sway over an unbelieving husband, imagine the influence it can exert upon a Christian husband who may not be obeying God's Word. Our submissive conduct actually provokes our husbands to be the leaders God intends for them to be.

For instance, have you ever had someone lean on you with his or her full body weight? What happened? Of course, your natural reaction was to exert the counter-pressure necessary to hold that person (and yourself) up! This is a picture of the effect of submission on our husbands. It places a godly pressure on them. It allows them to feel the full weight of their responsibility. More often than not, they rise to the challenge.

As Elizabeth George eloquently expresses it: "Our submission to our husband—whether or not he is a Christian, whether or not he is obeying God—preaches a lovelier and more powerful sermon than our mouth ever could!"[7]

OPENING OUR EYES TO RESPECT

Proceeding with our tour of 1 Peter 3:1-6, our next stop is in verse 2. Here Scripture specifies the attitude of our submissive conduct: It is to be "respectful and pure." Since chapter 5 of this book addresses purity, I will not elaborate on that topic further, but I would like to briefly consider the word *respect*.

If we peek ahead at verse 6 of 1 Peter 3, we see that Abraham's wife, Sarah, called him "lord." (Imagine how your husband would react if you greeted him in that fashion!) Although our application might be slightly different from Sarah's, the implication is clear: We are to show respect to our husbands. Ephesians 5:33 is even more straightforward: "Let the wife see that she respects her husband."

The definition of the Greek word for "respect" means "to be in awe of, to revere, or to treat as someone special." Is that how we act toward our husbands? Do we respect them with our words, tone of voice, countenance, and body language?

We must vigilantly study our husbands and perceive character traits worthy of respect, for how often are we guilty of overlooking numerous admirable qualities? Yet when we esteem our husbands, amazing results will follow! They will strive to be worthy of our respect, and simultaneously our own feelings of respect will grow.

Nancy Wilson observes, "It has been wisely stated, 'Obedience is the opener of eyes.' Discontent blinds women to the many good qualities in their husbands. [But] when gratitude and respect are cultivated for their husbands, wives find more and more to respect."[8]

So even if we do not feel particularly respectful today; or though we may not think our husbands have done anything worthy of respect lately; or even if we reckon ourselves to be more capable, intelligent, or godly than our husbands—none of these reasons exempt us. Respect is a decision we make to obey God's Word. He has set the husband as the head (1 Cor. 11:3), and we must honor that position regardless.

What grade would our husbands give us in the respect category? Let's not assume or speculate. We need to ask them! If we should get a "needs improvement" grade, let's work hard to bring up our score!

THE BEAUTY OF SUBMISSION

I want to tell you about an ancient beauty secret. It doesn't cost any money. There's no daily skin-care regimen or makeover necessary. It's not cosmetic surgery or an exotic spa treatment. But it has proven to be 100 percent effective for every woman who has ever tried it—no matter her age or physical appearance!

Do I have your attention yet?

Well, amazingly enough, this secret is found in God's Word, in 1 Peter 3:3-5. And this is why, without reservation, I can guarantee its effectiveness. Moving ahead on our tour to verse 5, we discover, "For this is how the holy women who hoped in God used to adorn themselves (or "make themselves beautiful," NIV), *by submitting to their husbands*" (emphasis mine).

Not only can submission woo an unbelieving husband to Christ; it can also make us beautiful! Now who of us doesn't want to be beautiful? As we see in these verses, first-century women desired to be beautiful as well. We can be grateful that the Bible doesn't overlook this subject. It unveils the virtue of submission as the secret to authentic, timeless beauty.

This beauty is not a physical beauty. As Paul tactfully puts it, "outwardly we are wasting away" (2 Cor. 4:16 NIV). Having reached middle age, I can certainly attest to that! Wrinkles are beginning to appear. It's harder to shed a few pounds. I'm experiencing aches and pains I never felt before. In short, it's all downhill from here.

So this 1 Peter 3 beauty secret is good news, for it promises that we will indeed grow lovelier as we cultivate submissive hearts. The verse doesn't reveal how this beauty develops. Nevertheless, this attractiveness is real, tangible, and visible to others. More significantly, it is a beauty "which in God's sight is very precious" (v. 4). Submission endows us with an altogether different kind of beauty, the kind that God sees and prizes—and the only kind of beauty that counts.

SUBMISSION MOMENTS

One of the countless things I love about my husband is his generosity. He is utterly unselfish when it comes to money and material possessions. Not only does he give lavishly to others, but he derives an exuberant delight from dispensing gifts where they are least expected! In most cases, I am eager to support his charitable habit. However, tension can sometimes arise when I think his giving exceeds our resources.

I remember a time when C. J. and I were having dinner at a local restaurant. I was already uneasy about the cost of the meal due to a temporary financial squeeze. *We should have stayed home and reheated leftovers*, I thought. But my anxiety level escalated when C. J. spied a couple from our church dining in the same restaurant and decided to pay for their meal as well!

Now C. J. always welcomes and often heeds my advice. So, as calmly as possible, I pointed out that perhaps we couldn't afford to be generous right now. But C. J. was not persuaded. He was determined to bless this couple, and I was faced with a "submission moment."

We all face moments like this! Our husbands make a decision or lead in a direction—and we don't agree. Maybe it just isn't our preference, or perhaps we think we have a better idea. Possibly, we fear it will result in adverse consequences. What enables us to submit at these times?

First Peter 3:5 provides the answer. It explains that holy women of the past "hoped in God." The same is true for us today. Our ability to submit proceeds from a resolute trust in God.

Scripture *doesn't* tell us to place our hope in our husbands. They are fallible, sinners—just as we are. They will make mistakes. Consequently, if we invest all our confidence in their leadership, character, or gifting, we will wind up anxious and disappointed. God never intended that our husbands bear the weight of our complete dependence. Rather, He wants us to depend wholly upon Him.

Submission, in its simplest form, is trust in God, who is completely trustworthy. He is our loving Father who controls every detail of our lives—past, present, and future. He lavishes us with goodness and blessing, and He measures our pain and adversity—all for our good and His glory.

As Jerry Bridges encourages us, "We can put this down as a bedrock truth: God will never allow any action against you that is not in accord with His will for you. And His will is always directed to our good."[9]

The question we must answer, then, is: *"Am I prepared to trust God to lead my husband, to lead me?"* As Susan Hunt says:

> The true woman is not afraid to place herself in a position of submission. She does not have to grasp; she does not have to control. Her fear dissolves in the light of God's covenant promise to be her God and to live within her. Submission is simply a demonstration of her confidence in the sovereign power of the Lord God.[10]

So how did God work in my submission moment, you might ask? Well, just a few days later, we received in the mail a gift certificate to the very same restaurant. We returned for another meal, but when we presented our gift certificate, the waitress informed us that we would need to come again to use it. Some friends in the restaurant had already picked up our tab. I sat there smiling to myself and thinking, *God, You always back this guy up!*

SARAH AND SUBMISSION

We have now arrived at the final destination on our 1 Peter 3 tour— verse 6. This is where we meet Sarah, our role model of wifely submission. In obedience to her husband, Abraham, Sarah accompanied him on a journey from their comfortable home in Ur to a distant, unknown land. For more than a decade of wandering, she trusted God to lead Abraham as they encountered many uncertain and unpleasant situations. But then Sarah failed a crucial submission moment.

She thought she had been patient—no, *very* patient! God had promised to grant her and Abraham a son, but Sarah was now approaching seventy-five years of age. Abraham still had no heir. So, she reasoned, it was time to take matters into her own hands.

Abandoning her trust in God, Sarah suggested to Abraham that it appeared unlikely God would fulfill His promise. Perhaps Abraham should take Sarah's maidservant, Hagar, as his wife and father a child by her. Abraham agreed, and Hagar bore him a son, Ishmael.

But what seemed like a prudent plan to Sarah had calamitous results. Hagar's pregnancy precipitated bitter conflict between Hagar, Sarah, and Abraham. This hostility extended to Ishmael and Isaac (the son Sarah would eventually bear) and ultimately evolved into the violent Arab-Israeli conflict we know today. Talk about failing a submission moment! Sarah's actions reaped dire consequences for generations to come.

Now don't you find it heartening that Peter singled out *Sarah* as our example of submission? She was not faultless in her dealings as Abraham's wife. She did not deliver a flawless performance of submission. And, of course, neither do we. But the fact that Scripture has not concealed her failures can bolster our own efforts to grow in submission.

Sarah's story doesn't end with her failure. By the time she gave birth to Isaac—a full fifteen years later—God had performed a momentous work of grace in her life. Her lack of trust in God matured into a robust faith. In fact, she is one of only two women listed among the Hebrews 11 "heroes of the faith." There we are informed that "by faith Sarah herself received power to conceive, even when she was past the age, *since she considered him faithful who had promised*" (v. 11, emphasis mine).

This God who transformed Sarah's disbelieving heart can do the same for us. If we embrace His plan for our lives and purpose to obey His commands, He will develop in us the beauty of submission. He will enable us to *trust Him to lead our husbands to lead us.*

9

Margaret's Story

I want to tell you about a woman named Margaret. Most likely you've never heard of her. She is not a champion of women's rights, a glamorous actress, or a recording artist. She isn't a successful businesswoman or politician. She's never authored a book or traveled the lecture circuit. She hasn't won any humanitarian awards or received academic honors. In fact, she never even went to college.

Margaret is simply a faithful wife and mother.

She has been married to her husband for almost sixty years. Together they raised five children—all of whom have families of their own now. Homemaking has been her sole career, and she poured her life into this calling.

A typical day for Margaret began before dawn. She fixed her husband's breakfast and packed his lunch for work. Then she woke her children and got them ready for school. The following hours were spent tackling an endless list of chores: laundry, ironing, mending, dusting the furniture, vacuuming the carpets, scrubbing the floors, cleaning the bathrooms, grocery shopping, errands, and cooking. By 5:30 P.M. she had dinner prepared for her family. Afterwards there were dishes to wash, household tasks to complete, baths for the little ones, homework help for the older ones, and nighttime stories to read. When she finally crawled into bed, only a precious few hours were afforded for sleep. Then it was time to start the routine all over again.

In this manner, Margaret tirelessly served her family—day after day, month after month, and year after year.

Now if you had the honor of meeting Margaret, you would at once be impressed by her joy. But her vivacious, delightful character is most conspicuous in the arena of her home. She's always smiling or singing. She is excited by the simplest of pleasures. She loves to laugh—so hard the tears run down her cheeks. And all through the years she marshaled this joyful energy for the well-being of her family. Never once did her children hear her complain. And not until they had children of their own did they comprehend the sacrifices she had made, for all her sacrifices had been masked by her perpetual joy.

Margaret's constant presence in the home provided comfort and security. Her children awoke each morning to the sound of her cheerful voice and returned home every afternoon to her warm greeting. She was always available—to hear about their days, call out study questions for a test, make them a snack, or bandage scraped knees. At no time was her family an interruption. She would drop whatever she was doing to tend to their most pressing concerns—without any mention of inconvenience. And if something was important or exciting to her husband or children, then it was of great interest to Margaret. Her life was intertwined with theirs. If they were happy, so was she. If they were suffering, so was she. No trial or joy was so small or insignificant as to escape her notice. Margaret's "being there"—not just physically but with all her heart—left an indelible imprint upon the members of her family.

Her lifelong service to her husband and children speaks most eloquently about her love for the Savior. God's love captured her heart as a teenager, and at the age of twenty-three she married a godly man. Together they imparted their love for God to their children. They modeled righteous character and genuine faith in the home. And they expressed that faith by commitment to their local church, a church they helped found almost fifty years ago. As Margaret's children will tell you—whenever the church doors were open, their entire family was present!

Margaret's gift of hospitality was an integral part of daily life in the church. Many a family enjoyed Sunday dinner at her home. As the hostess for numerous women's meetings at her house, she always prepared a vast array of refreshments. If a missionary family, guest speaker, or any visitor came into town, it was taken for granted that Margaret would host them. On one occasion, she even housed a choir! She would clean her small house, cook hearty meals, suggest outings for her guests, and even do their laundry. Along with her servanthood, her joyful demeanor made everyone feel at ease. So you can imagine why anyone visiting Margaret's home was eager to return again—and soon!

She freely extended hospitality in spite of her limited resources. Her husband was a construction worker, and though he eventually became a superintendent, Margaret had to manage the entire household with a mere forty dollars per week. But their financial situation did not deter her from giving. She would consistently set aside a portion of her weekly allowance and slip a small gift to someone facing hard times. For whether financial or practical, Margaret was always tuned in to the needs of others. If someone in the church was ill, in the hospital, or maybe just lonely, Margaret would visit the person. When a baby was born or a family member died, there was Margaret with a meal. For years she and her husband drove a disabled woman to and from the Sunday evening service.

Her charity did not end when she reached retirement age. In her late seventies she cared for a ninety-year-old widow by taking her to the doctor, the grocery store, or the hairdresser each week. Margaret was never enamored by popular or influential people. Rather, her heart was drawn like a magnet to anyone who was outcast, poor, or needy.

Those who lived near Margaret were also the recipients of her good deeds. She called her neighborhood "my little mission field." Whenever a new family moved in, Margaret would take them a meal. She and her husband frequently appeared on their neighbors' doorsteps with fresh-picked produce or homemade baked goods. Margaret also extended friendship to the women who lived around her. She supported and encouraged one young mom through seventeen years of mothering. Now this woman counts Margaret as dear as her own mother. And Margaret's like a grandma to all the neighborhood kids who loved to come to her house. She would listen to their tales, read them stories, and of course fix them a snack.

One young boy in particular loved to hang out at Margaret's house. He followed her around, talking to her while she cleaned. He stopped by early each morning when he walked his dog. He showed up at her door if he missed his bus and needed a ride to school. He even built a tree house on Margaret's property and would try to coax her to "come on up." So why, you might ask, would an active boy spend so much time with an elderly woman? Well, this child's mother was in prison, his father had deserted him, and he lived with his grandparents, who now had a second family to raise. Margaret's home was a place of refuge. No doubt her pleasant company and interest in his daily life provided much happiness and comfort for this lonely little boy.

But recently everything about Margaret's life has changed. Her husband suffered a stroke. She's eighty years old and unable to care for him on her own. So she's had to move—far from her home, her church, and her neighborhood—and take her husband to live with their daughter. Her days are now occupied with caring for this man she vowed to love—in sickness and in health—all the days of her life. She feeds him, bathes him, and reads to him from the Bible. Though she did not anticipate this abrupt turn of events, and despite the new and varied challenges before her, Margaret continues to serve faithfully.

But then serving has been a way of life for Margaret, and it's her servant's heart that has profoundly affected all who know her. While the orbit of her life was never very wide, to her husband, five children, and seventeen grandchildren, she means the world. Though she's lived in almost complete anonymity, her neighbors, young and old alike, will never forget her. She may not be extraordinarily gifted, but Margaret's fellow church members are eternally grateful for her sacrificial care.

Margaret has served without fanfare, never seeking attention or accolades. But one day soon, she will meet her Maker. On that day she will receive her "commendation from God." Although it's true, by worldly standards, that Margaret never accomplished anything great, in God's eyes she has achieved true greatness. Her life can be summed up by the words of our Lord: "Whoever would be great among you must be your servant . . . even as the Son of Man came not to be served but to serve, and to give his life as a ransom for many" (Matt. 20:26, 28).

Margaret is my example of a Titus 2 woman. Margaret is also my mom. And it's to you, Mom, that I lovingly dedicate this book.

Notes

ACKNOWLEDGMENTS

1. Anne Bradstreet, quoted in *365 Love Poems*, comp. John Gabriel Hunt (New York: Barnes & Noble, Inc. by arrangement with Random House Value Publishing, Inc., 1996), p. 172.

CHAPTER 1: TRANSFORMED BY TITUS 2

1. Elisabeth Elliot, "A Woman's Mandate," from *Family Practice*, ed. R. C. Sproul, Jr. (Phillipsburg, N.J.: P&R Publishing, 2001), p. 62.

CHAPTER 2: THE DELIGHT OF LOVING MY HUSBAND

1. "Do You Love Me?" from *Fiddler on the Roof*, copyright 1964 Sunbeam Music Corp. CCLI 105186. Based on the book by Joseph Stein. Lyrics by Sheldon Harnick.
2. Douglas Wilson, *Reforming Marriage* (Moscow, Ida.: Canon Press, 1995), p. 22.
3. Jonathan Edwards, *The Works of Jonathan Edwards, Volume 1* (Carlisle, Penn.: The Banner of Truth Trust, 1834, repr. 1987), p. xxii.
4. Charles Spurgeon, "Grace Quotes," e-mail publication, April 10, 2002, edited from Spurgeon's sermon "Ripe Fruit," #945.
5. Elisabeth Elliot, *Love Has a Price Tag* (Ann Arbor, Mich.: Servant Books, 1979), p. 97.
6. Shirley Rice, quoted in Ed Wheat, *Love Life for Every Married Couple* (Grand Rapids, Mich.: Zondervan Publishing House, 1980), pp. 87-88.
7. Linda Dillow, *Creative Counterpart* (Nashville, Tenn.: Thomas Nelson Publishers, 1986), p. 120.
8. Charles Spurgeon, *Morning and Evening* (Peabody, Mass.: Hendrickson Publishers, 1995), p. 551.

CHAPTER 3: THE BLESSINGS OF LOVING MY CHILDREN

1. Katrina Kenison, *Mitten Strings for God* (New York: Warner Books, 2000), p. 171.
2. Stephen and Janet Bly, *How to Be a Good Mom* (Chicago: Moody Press, 1988), p. 13.
3. Charles Bridges, *Proverbs* (Carlisle, Penn.: The Banner of Truth Trust, 1846, repr. 1994), p. 323.
4. Kenison, *Mitten Strings for God*, p. 217.
5. John Charles Ryle, *The Duties of Parents* (Conrad, Mont.: Triangle Press, 1994), pp. 8-9.

6. John Angell James, *Female Piety* (Morgan, Penn.: Soli Deo Gloria Publications, 1860, repr. 1995), p. 316.

7. Joyce Maynard, *Domestic Affairs* (New York: McGraw-Hill Book Company, 1988), p. 9.

CHAPTER 4: THE SAFETY OF SELF-CONTROL

1. Charles Bridges, *Proverbs* (Carlisle, Penn.: The Banner of Truth Trust, 1846, repr. 1994), pp. 483-484.

2. Jerry Bridges, *The Practice of Godliness* (Colorado Springs, Colo.: NavPress Publishing Group, 1996), p. 132.

3. Elisabeth Elliot, *Discipline, The Glad Surrender* (Old Tappan, N.J.: Fleming H. Revell, 1982), p. 45.

4. Elyse Fitzpatrick, *Love to Eat, Hate to Eat* (Eugene, Ore.: Harvest House Publishers, 1999), p. 93.

5. Martha Peace, *Becoming a Titus 2 Woman* (Bemidji, Minn.: Focus Publishing, Inc., 1997), pp. 116-117.

6. Martyn Lloyd-Jones, *Spiritual Depression: Its Causes and Cure* (Grand Rapids, Mich.: Wm. B. Eerdmans, 1965, repr. 2001), p. 20.

7. C. S. Lewis, from a letter to Sheldon Vanauken in Vanauken's *A Severe Mercy* (New York: Harper and Row, 1977), p. 189.

8. Charles Spurgeon, *Morning and Evening* (Peabody, Mass.: Hendrickson Publishers, 1995), p. 49.

9. John Blanchard, *How to Enjoy Your Bible* (Faverdale North, Darlington, UK: Evangelical Press, 1993).

CHAPTER 5: THE PLEASURE OF PURITY

1. Daniel L. Akin, "Sermon: The Beauty and Blessings of the Christian Bedroom, Song of Solomon 4:1—5:1," *The Southern Baptist Journal of Theology*, Vol. 6, No. 1, Spring 2002, p. 94.

2. Ruth Smythers, "Instruction and Advice for the Young Bride," *The Madison Institute Newsletter*, Fall 1894, copyright 1894 by The Madison Institute (New York: Spiritual Guidance Press).

3. Glenda Revell, *Glenda's Story: Led by Grace* (Lincoln, Neb.: Gateway to Joy, 1997), p. 41.

4. Ibid., p. 98.

5. Anne Atkins, *The Daily Telegraph*, quoted by John Hosier in a sermon, "Being Servants of God," at Newfrontiers Leaders' and Wives' Conference, 1999.

6. Elisabeth Elliot, *Passion and Purity* (Grand Rapids, Mich.: Fleming H. Revell, division of Baker Book House, 2000), p. 26.

7. Charles Spurgeon, *Psalms,* Vol. 2, The Crossway Classic Commentaries, Alister McGrath and J. I. Packer, eds. (Wheaton, Ill.: Crossway Books, 1993), p. 61.

8. William Shakespeare, *Much Ado About Nothing*, Shakespeare.com, copyright 2000 by Dana Spradley, publisher. Originally taken from *Complete Moby Shakespeare*.

9. Source unknown.

10. Elisabeth Elliot, *Let Me Be a Woman* (Wheaton, Ill.: Tyndale House, 1987), pp. 169-170.

11. Akin, "Beauty and Blessings," *Southern Baptist Journal of Theology*, p. 98.

12. Robert Farrar Capon, quoted in Debra Evans, *The Mystery of Womanhood* (Wheaton, Ill.: Crossway Books, 1987), p. 265.

CHAPTER 6: THE HONOR OF WORKING AT HOME

1. Danielle Crittenden, *What Our Mothers Didn't Tell Us* (New York: Simon & Schuster, 1999), p. 22.

2. Ibid., p. 122.

3. Louis Uchitelle, "Job Track or 'Mommy Track'? Some Do Both, in Phases," *The New York Times*, July 5, 2002.

4. F. Carolyn Graglia, *Domestic Tranquility* (Dallas, Tex.: Spence Publishing, 1998), p. 92.

5. Dorothy Patterson, *Where's Mom?* (Wheaton, Ill.: Crossway Books, 2003), p. 21.

6. Crittenden, *What Our Mothers Didn't Tell Us*, p. 13.

7. William J. Petersen, *Martin Luther Had a Wife* (Wheaton, Ill.: Tyndale House, 1983), p. 14.

8. Ibid., p. 81.

9. Patterson, *Where's Mom?*, p. 45.

10. Douglas Wilson, *Reforming Marriage* (Moscow, Ida.: Canon Press, 1995), p. 16.

11. Jean Brand, *A Woman's Privilege* (London: Triangle, 1985), p. 120.

12. Dawson Trotman, "Born to Reproduce" (Lincoln, Neb.: Back to the Bible). Etext by The Christian Digital Library Foundation, Inc., http://www.atl.mindspring.com/~iom

13. Mary Pride, *The Way Home* (Wheaton, Ill.: Crossway Books, 1985), p. 202.

14. Catherine Marshall, *A Man Called Peter* (New York: McGraw-Hill, 1961), p. 65.

CHAPTER 7: THE REWARDS OF KINDNESS

1. Jerry Bridges, *The Practice of Godliness* (Colorado Springs, Colo.: NavPress Publishing Group, 1996), p. 189.

2. Robert D. Jones, "Learning Contentment in All Your Circumstances," *The Journal of Biblical Counseling*, Vol. 21, No. 1, Fall 2002, p. 58.

3. I am indebted to Dr. David Powlison for this illustration.

4. David Powlison, "Anger, Part 1: Understanding Anger," *The Journal of Biblical Counseling*, Vol. 14, No. 1, Fall 1995, p. 42.

5. David Powlison, "How Shall We Cure Troubled Souls?" in *The Coming Evangelical Crisis*, John H. Armstrong, ed. (Chicago: Moody Press, 1996), p. 212.

6. Jim Wilson, *How to Be Free from Bitterness* (Moscow, Ida.: Canon Press, 1995), p. 9.

7. C. J. Mahaney, *The Cross Centered Life* (Sisters, Ore.: Multnomah Publishers, 2002), p. 81.

8. Valerie Cox, "The Cookie Thief," in Jack Canfield and Mark Victor Hansen, *A 3rd Serving of Chicken Soup for the Soul* (Deerfield Beach, Fla.: Health Communications, 1996).

9. Ken Sande, "Judging Others: The Danger of Playing God," *The Journal of Biblical Counseling*, Vol. 21, No. 1, Fall 2002, p. 13.

10. Bill Keane, "The Family Circus," in *Chicken Soup for the Mother's Soul* (Deerfield Beach, Fla.: Health Communications, 1997), p. 147.

11. Charles Spurgeon, *Spurgeon at His Best* (Grand Rapids, Mich.: Baker Book House, 1991), p. 143.

12. John Bunyan, quoted in Randy Alcorn, *In Light of Eternity* (Colorado Springs, Colo.: Waterbrook Press, 1999), p. 120.

CHAPTER 8: THE BEAUTY OF SUBMISSION

1. Wayne Grudem, "Gender Confusion: The Way Forward," sermon given at Newfrontiers Brighton Leadership Conference, 2002.

2. Wayne Grudem, "The Key Issues in the Manhood-Womanhood Controversy," *Building Strong Families*, ed. Dennis Rainey (Wheaton, Ill.: Crossway Books, 2002), p. 61.

3. Elisabeth Elliot, "Notes on Submission," *The Elisabeth Elliot Newsletter*, September/October 2002 (Ann Arbor, Mich.: Servant Ministries).

4. John Piper, "A Vision of Biblical Complementarity: Manhood and Womanhood Defined According to the Bible," *Recovering Biblical Manhood and Womanhood*, John Piper and Wayne Grudem, eds. (Wheaton, Ill.: Crossway Books, 1991), p. 53.

5. As quoted in Sinclair B. Ferguson, *Deserted by God?* (Grand Rapids, Mich.: Baker Books, 1993), p. 16.

6. Elliot, "Notes on Submission," *Elisabeth Elliot Newsletter*.

7. Elizabeth George, *A Woman After God's Own Heart* (Eugene, Ore.: Harvest House Publishers, 1997), p. 69.

8. Nancy Wilson, *The Fruit of Her Hands* (Moscow, Ida.: Canon Press, 1997), p. 33.

9. Jerry Bridges, *Trusting God* (Colorado Springs, Colo.: NavPress, 1988), p. 71.

10. Susan Hunt, *The True Woman* (Wheaton, Ill.: Crossway Books, 1997), p. 223.

More Resources from Carolyn Mahaney

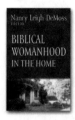

Biblical Womanhood in the Home

Crossway Books
Carolyn contributed two chapters to this volume compiled by
Nancy Leigh DeMoss—"Femininity: A Biblical Perspective,"
and "True Beauty." She is among seven beloved teachers (Mary
Kassian, P. Bunny Wilson, Barbara Hughes, Susan Hunt,
Dorothy Patterson, and Nancy DeMoss), each with a different
perspective on biblical womanhood. Their common thread is
joy and delight in the greatness of God's created order and the
part women play in his grand redemptive plan. The chapters are
based on messages these women gave a few years ago at a conference hosted by FamilyLife Ministries and the Council on
Biblical Manhood and Womanhood (CBMW). Available in
your local Christian bookstore.

Mothers & Daughters

Sovereign Grace Ministries —AUDIO SERIES—
This presentation by Carolyn and her daughters (Nicole
Whitacre, Kristin Chesemore, and Janelle Bradshaw), was originally given to the women's ministry at Covenant Life Church,
where Carolyn's husband, C.J., serves as senior pastor. In these
three messages, Carolyn sets forth a mother's responsibility to
her daughter, and her three daughters discuss a daughter's
proper response. Includes a live question and answer session.
Available on CD or cassette from the Sovereign Grace Store
(www.sovereigngracestore.com).

A Song of Joy: Romance and Sexual Intimacy in Marriage

Sovereign Grace Ministries —AUDIO SERIES—
Romance and sexual intimacy are gifts that God has given to
married couples—gifts to be treasured, pursued, and enjoyed
for as long as they both shall live. Here in five compelling messages from C.J. and Carolyn Mahaney is wise, godly, encouraging counsel, drawn from the *Song of Songs* and applicable to
every Christian marriage. Available on CD or cassette from the
Sovereign Grace Store (www.sovereigngracestore.com).

Additional messages from Carolyn Mahaney

Sovereign Grace Ministries
The Sovereign Grace Store also features individual messages from Carolyn, including "What to Do About the Things You Can't Do Anything About," "In Every Season of Life," "Being Careful How We Live," and "Hannah: From Misery to Joy."

Recommended Music

Upward: The Bob Kauflin Hymns Project

Sovereign Grace Music
This project is from the principal worship leader in Carolyn's home church. Bob Kauflin (a founding member of GLAD) selected, adapted, and arranged these songs—some of them familiar, some new, and some newly revised. Featuring diverse musical styles, plus a devotional from Bob for each song, this collection contains life-changing truth for all ages. *Upward* is one of many worship releases from Sovereign Grace Music (formerly PDI Music). Visit the Sovereign Grace website to listen to song samples www.sovereigngraceministries.org/music). To order, go to the Sovereign Grace Store (www.sovereigngrace-store.com).